THE ART OF SELLING
CYBER
SECURITY

MAHDI RAZA   DAVID MAHDI

I wrote this book hoping to inspire change.
If I have inspired you, I have succeeded.

ACKNOWLEDGEMENTS

This book would not have been possible without the help of some remarkable people.

Firstly, David Mahdi, my co-author, your guidance and advice was invaluable in shaping this book.

To the phenomenal contributor's Victoria Vuong, Kush Sharma, George Al-Koura, Hashim Hussein, Mansoor Khan, Daniel Pinsky, John Pinard, Ali Khan, Abbas Kudrati, Ketan Kapadia, Karen Nemani, Daniel Ehrenreich & Ali Hirji, you all brought thought leadership to help develop the book.

To my great editors, Zareen Zaidi, Zainab Zaidi & Ali-Akber Raza thank you for being great. I am grateful for your review and improvements. A special thanks to the final editor, Hina Ali, your final edits made this book complete. Fatima Alsammak, thank you for making this book visually fun to read.

Forever grateful to all of you.

PREFACE

Welcome!

You're reading this book because you are looking for something to take you from what currently is to what can be. I want to be the first one to congratulate you on prioritizing your worth and investing in yourself. Before getting into the specifics of Cybersecurity, I wanted to ensure you are entering this journey with the right mindset.

One of the most rewarding aspects of my career, specifically in cyber, has been sharing insight and advice on what has arguably become the most frequently asked question to a classic problem in sales. It's none other than the "help me; I just can't sell" plea. What follows is the, how do you sell? How do you not sell? What do you do? What can I do, and so on.

I've had the privilege of meeting some of the brightest and most curious minds. Whether through a casual conversation at a ball game or a mentorship training program, I'm often responding to requests for career-related advice on success with selling and barbecuing, but let's leave that for another book.

As the world shut down during the global pandemic, I found myself welcoming an opportunity to help myself help you. So here I am writing the book that you just can't put down (that is a good thing).

Keep reading because, by the time you are done reading this book, you will be equipped with winning strategies and information that will empower you to break through the challenges that cybersecurity salespeople relentlessly face.

This book amalgamates the best strategies, knowledge, skills, ideas, techniques and concepts that sales leaders use every day. Everything you need to learn to win will be presented throughout the pages of this book. Before diving into the nitty and gritty, three essential components serve as the prerequisite to any form of success. Those are courage, passion and intelligence. These are what I like to call the *soul of success*.

You can dedicate your life to absorbing the content from books, world-renowned speakers and experts, but if you deprive your soul of its success (courage, passion and intelligence), you will remain stagnant. Having the fastest horse without its jockey will not win any races and having information without the application of your soul is no different. Knowing what courage is, understanding how important passion is and applying the intelligence within you are the three fundamental requirements for every human striving towards success. To be excellent, not only do you need to know what these are, but you have to live them.

Live courageously.

Live passionately.

Live intelligently.

Courage, passion and intelligence are the most prominent core attributes of every successful human being.

In 2021, several reports showed that the market size for cybersecurity sales is about $200 billion US and is expected to double by 2025.[1] The rapid adoption of healthcare and other government-led industries has made the long-overdue cybersecurity conversation relevant and real.

There is an undeniable need for the successful application of cybersecurity, and the first step is to make it available through the art of selling cybersecurity.

There is power in sharing stories and experiences, especially from life lessons. To be completely honest, my life lessons have inspired me to

1   Hurst, Aaron. 2021. "Cyber security spending heading for $200 billion a year — Bloomberg." Information Age. https://www.information-age.com/cyber-security-spending-heading-for-200-billion-year-bloomberg-123494864/

write this book, hoping that it will positively impact those who read it. I hope it will be a simple yet impactful contribution to improving our world.

I have had the privilege to learn from some incredible sources and fantastic people. If my unique collection of experiences can provide even one hopeful individual with the opportunity to improve their life and the quality of HOW they live it, I have achieved my goal, and this book will not have been written in vain.

By now, your mindset should be activated. You will carry the courage, passion, and intelligence that I defined earlier.

Know it. Absorb it. Own it.

ESTABLISH YOUR INTENTION

"Losing sight of your intention is losing sight of yourself."
Mahdi Raza.

Before you begin anything, make it a habitual ritual to establish your intention. Whether going into a difficult meeting or preparing to host a large gathering, ask yourself your intention. Setting an intention leads to a cognitive awareness that subconsciously impacts the behaviours that follow. You ensure your thoughts, words, and actions stay aligned with the journey when you know your goal. On the contrary, you settle to stay in an unaware state when you have not established an intention. The risk of conducting yourself this way is that no intention can lead to a negative intention opposite of what you would have liked.

Intention goes beyond the simple sales goal. Every salesperson enters a sale with the intent to succeed. However, more than one intention lies in success. Small intentions are required, that together, lead to a general "my intention is to get the sale" plan. Pay attention to the multiple opportunities to establish intention in the little things because together they will create a successful plan.

For example, perhaps you are conducting a follow-up call post-sale. What is your intention? Is it to remind the client that you still exist? If so, what are you going to say? Align your thoughts and words accordingly. Is it to present a new and exciting product that you know, based on your understanding of their business, will provide value to their current goal? What are you going to say, and in what order? Or perhaps you intend to practice your ability to handle objection responses. What you think and plan to say and do will determine your ability to maintain integrity towards your intention.

Understanding your intention will influence how you speak, the words you choose, the energy you emit will be authentic, and it will flow naturally, almost effortlessly. Not only that, but your energy will also be contagious, which can be a beautiful thing.

As you read through this book, ensure you understand your intention. Think about that. Establish it. Then, absorb the content of these pages with your unique intention.

CONTENTS

CHAPTER ONE

INTRODUCTION TO CYBERSECURITY SALES

"It's not about closing a sale; it's about opening a relationship."

Daniel Pinsky

We are all part of the sales process.

Whether you are selling an idea, perhaps a widget/product, or your services, it all comes down to whether you believe you are "the one"? It's a yes or no question. If you do, then congratulations; you just might have a chance at realizing your potential. If you don't, worry not; you are in the right place, so keep reading.

What are sales? In its simplest definition, a sale is an exchange of one thing for another. A "salesperson" facilitates that exchange.

When you were a toddler and wanted a toy or a candy, if you didn't get it, guess what you did? You would cry, beg, or use any tactic in your toddler toolkit and turn it into your superpower until you achieved your goal. Eventually, as you grew and as your intellect evolved, you started using new and improved methods to convince your parents, siblings and friends to buy into whatever you wanted. Humans are always innately selling, whether it was with your teacher, trying to get an extra one per cent on your final exam, or closing a $5,000,000 deal. It's ingrained in our DNA, and for some, it flows a lot more naturally than it does for others.

Stay with me on this short journey as I demystify the art of selling and enlighten you with the selling techniques that you never knew you needed. This rewarding experience will teach you how to enhance your inner selling capabilities.

The selling process is pretty much the same every single time. The only variable that changes is the product or service.

To become a confident cybersecurity salesperson, you will have to apply the methodologies presented consistently in this book. The tips and tricks I will introduce to you will up your game!

David Mahdi, the co-author of this book, states:

> *While different industries have varying nuances concerning selling, in this book, we focus on growing in a fast-paced industry of cybersecurity. The cybersecurity industry is certainly not for the faint of heart.*

The above is especially true as the threats change daily, exacerbating the stress on CISOs and security teams. As such, sales approaches and strategies must account for the rapidly changing dynamics in the cybersecurity space. The focus and differentiation are its focus on the fast-moving cybersecurity market. Selling here requires a balance of timing and a level of technical understanding. And while there are several sales publications readily available, in this short yet powerful book, I will share the skills and help you find your confidence in selling cybersecurity.

When it comes to sales in business, the external factors and internal feelings are challenged because it's no longer mom and dad that you're trying to convince to buy you that new car for university. I live by the fundamental fact that only one type of sale occurs; either you sell to the person to purchase that product/service, or they sell you on why they do not want it.

Sales is a significant function in any organization that generates revenue which most people find challenging to master. Some say it's 'the' function. The reality is that an organization is heavily dependent on its revenue resulting from sales.

It is no secret that the most sought-after roles tend to be the Chief Technology Officer (CTO), Chief Financial Officer (CFO), Chief Information Security Officer (CISO), Chief Executive Officer (CEO), versus the Chief Sales/Revenue Officer. The truth is that the product or service your team has worked on will not generate any revenue until you can successfully persuade the prospective end-users to buy it.

Mastering the art of sales and acquiring relevant skills are vital to every cybersecurity salesperson. This is essentially what will close the deal every time.

THE SALES BURGER

"The key to successful sales involves determining the problem that needs to be solved and developing a solution to resolve the problem. Any successful product delivers a solution to a problem. People will buy things because they resolve their problem, not just because it is 'cool' or it has a great marketing plan. To summarize, find a solution to your customer's problem, and they will gladly pay your price."

John Pinard

The number one mistake people make when trying to sell something is that they do not have a linear process to get from point A to point Z.

Karen Nemani puts it best when she says: *cybersecurity sales can no longer rely on FUD – Fear Uncertainty and Doubt – as a tool to convince organizations they need the security solution you're proposing. In today's world, business owners want to know how your security product or service will not only secure their business and solve their problem but they also want to know how your solution will enable their business to grow and achieve current and future goals.*

In the bestseller, "Made to Stick" by Chip and Dan Heath, the author points out that leveraging common and existing concepts is a powerful approach to teaching new concepts to a broad audience.[2]

Here's a fun fact: Bringing food into a business meeting will have everyone racing towards it. There's something about food that just makes

2   Heath, Dan. 2007. *Made to Stick: Why Some Ideas Survive and Others Die.* Edited by Random House. N.p.: Random House Publishing Group.

everyone so happy. In the spirit of that, let's jazz it up for a moment and shift our focus towards the success of McDonald's good ol' BigMac burger. Have you ever wondered why a McDonald's BigMac is the exact same BigMac regardless of where on the planet you order it? Whether in San Francisco or Singapore, McDonald's has perfected their BigMac. How did McDonald's perfect the famous BigMac on a global scale?

It's pretty simple. They adopted, what I like to call, a "relentless repeatable process" approach to their business.

Let's take this analogy of a famous burger to understand the fundamental processes in selling.

To simplify this, we will start by breaking it down: the bottom of the bun is innovation, the meat is sales, and the top bun is marketing.

THE CYBERSECURITY SALES BURGER

BOTTOM BUN

INNOVATION & AGILITY: Innovation requires agility; it is the catalyst driving innovation. A cyber sales professional's greatest asset is using agile methods in innovation processes. Think of Cybersecurity as a super-fast supercar. You need to adapt to drive safely and quickly. Innovation comes in different forms and various degrees. It can mean new products and solutions, new marketing ideas, or new strategies. I can add more to this list, and I still would not have scratched the surface. However, this book is focused on how to sell cybersecurity. So, I will share a high-level understanding of why innovation is the *lifeline* of sales. And yes, it *all* starts with creativity.

Often underestimated, creativity is a super skill that enables you to adapt your sales process. Adaptability is never-ending, and committing to the evolution of your creative aptitude is the leverage you want to retain. Creativity is your inner craft. Investing in the growth of your craft has a direct impact on your sales capability. So tap into your creative side, and if you don't have one, try searching into that part of your brain and find it — it will enhance and unlock creativity that you didn't even know you had.

Get to know yourself. Find your colour and feel your beat. Turn off all that you see and turn on all that you think. Take a cooking class, explore art, or participate in something that helps you move to the beat of

CYBERSECURITY SALES BURGER

MARKETING

SALES

INNOVATION

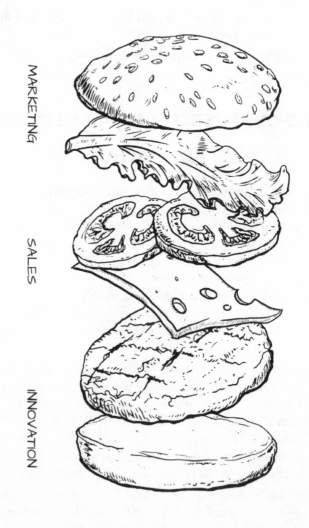

your soul instead of thoughts. Spend a day hiking and taking in all there is to experience alongside the hills and mountains. Meditate. Write. Paint. The outlets available are innumerable. Do what you need to do to unlock your mind's native, creative part. Find your creative spark and let your creativity do the talking. Before you say you can't, know that I have met people who firmly say, "I can't be creative" my response has always been, "I don't believe it." I say this with a pinch of salt because I believe that creativity is part of everyone's persona. Some just don't know that side of themself yet. Everyone carries a creative capacity. Tapping into that beautiful and unique energy and applying it is how you accelerate in the supercar that is you.

If innovation had a twin, it would be the solving of problems. Identifying a problem is one thing, but our DNA is part of our desire to solve problems. We were born to find solutions. Remember the glory of our youth when we convinced our parents to buy us the toy we wanted. Our creativity showed us that we needed that specific toy to solve the problem, which was the void we'd have without it.

Creativity is innovation. Innovation is hacking.

As David says, *"innovation will mean adapting and being agile to a changing landscape."*

Karen Nemani adds, *"innovation incorporates the ability to look at something with a different lens and finding new opportunities as a result. This is why diversity of thought and experience is critical to successful innovation."*

I couldn't agree more! It's a circle of life. ABC — Always Be Creative!

KEY TAKEAWAY: While 'innovation' will mean different things to different people, it is simply making progress, moving forward, or trying something new or better. It does not necessarily happen in a particular magnitude, and the effect can be felt regardless of which form or manner it takes. To every problem, there is a solution, and that solution is innovation.

THE MEAT

SALES: The fundamental goal, motivation, and desired outcome of selling is revenue generation. Making MONEY period.

Lucky for you, I can show you the way to that cash stash.

Selling involves reaching out to prospective clients and providing solutions to problems they may or may not be aware of. Issues that require the answer you have available, especially for them. It is the art of demonstrating the value that will sell your security product or service and gain a subscription to your mailing list.

This is the catalyst in selling. Learn this and master it. When you do, achieving sales targets will flow naturally.

The Gartner 2022 Chief Sales officer poll revealed the topmost priorities of sales organizations in the United States; that is, the development of a new sales pipeline and activating virtual selling.[3]

Hubspot defines sales as: *a term that describes every activity that culminates into selling a product or service.*[4]

Suppose we combine Hubspot's definition of sales with what CISOs and security leaders are presently prioritizing. In that case, we can understand sales to be the act of developing a new sales pipeline and leveraging virtual selling. It constantly evolves and adapts to innovative tools and technologies to convert prospective leads into revenue-generating clients.

Fishing for sales is the delicate balance of patience and persistence. It's what keeps the best fisherman afloat, happily and successfully sailing!

Here is some great advice from Kush Sharma, an experienced public sector cybersecurity leader:

Sales is key, especially when trying to sell to the government. You must understand that the motivations and drivers are different from the private sector.

In most governments, the budget cycles are fixed once approved. Understanding when budget discussions begin and when the final ap-

---

3   "Top Priorities for Chief Sales Officers & Leaders in 2022." n.d. Gartner. Accessed March 22, 2022. https://www.gartner.com/en/sales/insights/sales-leaders-top-priorities.

4   Hart, Meredith. 2022. "What Is Sales? A Quick Guide [+ Examples]." HubSpot Blog. https://blog.hubspot.com/sales/what-is-sales.

proval is given is key to successfully selling. If you miss this window, you may have to wait until the next budget cycle the following year. It is an exercise in long-term relationship building and upfront investment. Being patient with a mid/long-term strategy and persistent in building relationships, networking and education/awareness are fundamental table-stakes to achieving a successful close.

For example, each government entity has its own procurement rules, timelines, requirements, and processes. Conducting a deep dive and understanding these are half the battle. Not all government entities use the same bid solicitation platform, complicating the process administratively. You must first understand which platform your target entity uses as a precursor to your sales strategy. If you cast your fishing net wide, subscribing to all the relevant platforms may be the only approach.

Before submitting your bid, you may want to ask the right questions to provide a more accurate cost estimate. However, note that any responses provided by the government entity will be shared with all bidders. Typically, organizations with existing contracts and knowledge would not ask many questions as it would be disadvantageous to disclose additional information to their competition. Alternatively, smaller organizations or new bidders hoping to land their first deal may want to ask more questions to understand the current environment better and/or clarify expectations.

Note that the cost evaluation often holds considerable weight due to funding challenges. Also, be very particular in ensuring that every question/section of the RFP is responded to in as much detail as possible. Not providing the expected responses may lead you to lose points during the evaluation. Why? Because evaluation teams are usually managed by non-technical procurement specialists that follow the evaluation criteria and score to a tee. They are not Cybersecurity experts.

Kush Sharma has given you a great understanding of the procurement vehicles and timing and knowledge.

I asked Karen Nemani what the top two ways to get your foot in the public sector door are and she mentioned the following:

1. Operational plans (4-5 year plans are created and updated yearly) and strategic priorities;

2. Political climate. In this, I mean take a peek at the timeline to an election and ensure you have an understanding of what priorities remain on the political table that the party committed to yet haven't delivered. Knowing these are key to putting together a procurement package of talent or product that would have the government procurement folks come find you and select your organization out of all the others instead of you chasing them.

We will continue to dig deeper into sales throughout the next chapters and rest assured, you will learn what it takes for you to be the best cybersecurity salesperson, but right now, we've got to take care of this burger business.

Remember, it's "Bun. Meat. Bun." Without the meat, there is no burger.

KEY TAKEAWAY: Sales are driven by hunger. How hungry are you to achieve your goals? Do you wake up in the morning believing that you will close deals? Patience and persistence are critical elements that come hand in hand. You should also be using multi-channel strategies and never be idle.

TOP OF THE BUN

MARKETING

Picture this; its mid-afternoon on a Monday morning. You're tired because you just can't seem to get to bed early on Sunday nights no matter what. As you're driving to work, moving at snail speed, bumper to bumper, of course, you start creating a mental list of the things you plan to accomplish on this very predictable Monday. Of course, you will finish the reports and presentation prep and get as much done as humanly possible, but the most important decision to take is 'what's for lunch?' It takes you less than half a second to commit to a burger from your favourite burger joint. You start visualizing it as you peek at the other drivers in their cars, also driving at a snail's speed. That beautiful bun that you love to love is perfect. The bun to meat ratio balances just like Sonny and Cher did every time they sang "I got you, babe," and you know instantly that this burger has got you. Your Monday morning just went from mundane and redundant to "this is going to be a beautiful day" all because of your burger and that beautiful bun that hugs all those meat and condiment details into one glorious declaration of excellence, delivered right into your hungry (possibly hangry) Monday morning lunch belly.

Now that I have your attention, I'm sure you will be sneaking away into your favourite burger joint soon. Sneak away, my friends! Before you do, though, understand that the reason why you are going to need that burger is that the bun just sold you.

Let's discuss! Marketing is the top bun in the sales burger analogy. Just like the bun, marketing is a pretty big deal! It is the romance before the marriage proposal, and it is everything! Through marketing, you showcase the value of why your end-users need your products and services. Your end-user will be in a "you complete me" Jerry Maguire state of love when done effectively.

So how is effective marketing done? How do you persuade someone to buy into the neatly packaged box you are selling them? A few pages ago, I encouraged you to pay attention to your creative aptitude and let it bloom. Creativity is a major game-changer when it comes to marketing. You've got to package the features and benefits of your product and services skillfully, precisely and artfully, and if the bun is on point, your prospective customer will be craving that sales burger. I don't know about you, but there's something about burgers that fills me up with love. In the spirit of love: Think back to when you wanted to woo a special somebody you didn't know but knew you wanted to know. That wanting to know turned into a passionate need to know. The need to know unleashed the courage to walk right up to that special somebody. The conversation that took place after was your intelligence taking the lead and securing your Friday night date for the many Fridays that would follow because you were just that smooth.

HOW DID YOU SCORE THAT FIRST DATE?

Let's examine the anatomy of your marketable variables for a moment.

Okay, so you knew you had to get your person of interest to be interested in you, so you made it a point to investigate and understand what would get their attention.

You knew wearing khakis and a collared shirt wouldn't cut it because you wanted to avoid being Mr. Bean, so you went and got yourself the coolest kicks from Athlete's World because that's what you did in the '90s (and since I am writing this book, we will go with the 90's because it was arguably one of the best decades ever, although the '80s come pretty close).

Anyway, back to the prep. So, you got those kicks and then went home and coordinated the perfect outfit the night before. Dark blue jeans and a slick t-shirt would casually draw attention to the countless hours you spent at the gym chiselling out the fabulous in you, *and what a work of art you were, Michelangelo!*

You knew your special somebody loved chocolate, so you picked up a KitKat and rehearsed what you planned on saying, which was none other than "take a break this Friday, have dinner with me."

You wanted to capitalize on every resource available, and the (sing this next part with me) *"gimme a break, gimme a break, break me off a piece of that KitKat bar"* advertisement offered the perfect rom-com flare. You worked your creativity, and it was going to be magical!

You woke up on game day early in the morning, 20 minutes earlier, because styling your John Stamos hair was critical, and the gel needed its own time to set.

You put on your game day tune, which was none other than "Eye of the Tiger" because it worked for Rocky.

You got into your outfit and misted yourself in a solid two to ten sprays of your signature scent. You understood the power of being resourceful and leveraging everything at your disposal. Now you looked good, and thanks to Calvin Klein, you smelled as impressive as the '90s did.

Finally, when the moment arrived, you grew a few inches taller because your posture was as sharp as it had ever been. Your walk was on fire, and you had a pep in each step. You owned every second of that walk, and your eyes began to speak as soon as you made eye contact with your KitKat catch.

And guess what? You were irresistibly delicious. You captured their attention like a boss. All this happened before you even said a word.

With the hook in, all you had to do was fancy them with a little subtle persuasion and close the Friday night plan, and because you already understood them, you knew what approach to use.

You charmed your way through that conversation using your humour, wit and confidence. Your words were hypnotic, and then boom, they accepted your invitation to be the favourite part of your Friday night.

You made a sensible choice to offer a low-risk date night, not a marriage proposal that would probably have resulted in a restraining order.

Creating a stellar marketing concept is about figuring out what your target client likes and dislikes. What can you provide that will make them happy, and how do you speak to them in a language they will understand and welcome?

Cybersecurity sales are heavily dependent on relationship building. Promoting the products and services relevant to the client's unique needs is imperative. Moving them through the sales channels will all flow naturally with successful marketing.

Through the KitKat catch romance above, you immediately see the power of:

1. Capturing your target market's attention.

2. Persuading them to buy your product.

3. Offering them a specific, low-risk action (cybersecurity example: downloading a free eBook or white paper or even subscribing to your mailing list).

Remember, it's not the 90s, and as such, you don't need to be standing next to your target to engage in meaningful communication. Use the endless channels available to you in a way that makes sense to your client, whether it's through social media, events, advertising, sales, virtual sessions, roundtables, LinkedIn, or siberXchange. Wherever the doorbell is, ring it and enable yourself to be heard.

CHAPTER TWO

SALES AND MARKETING CHANNELS IN THE CYBERSECURITY INDUSTRY

"Marketing messages are often technical and confusing. The Marketing message or slogan should be plain English and easy to understand. Any business executive or CISO should be able to grasp what you're trying to sell quickly. Avoid using too many acronyms. Recently, I had a meeting with a software supply chain security vendor. After 20 minutes into their technical presentation, I paused and summarized their new technology in one sentence" - 'a SOAR for application security.' Keep it simple."

Kush Sharma

I recently watched the finale of Gordon Ramsay's *Next Level Chef*. The show's premise was based on contestants striving to thrive in an unexpected environment with limited time and resources. Each week, a contestant would walk into the game without knowing what type of kitchen they would be in. They had only a minute to grab the ingredients they could use, and with that, they would create the best meal they possibly could. They would focus on everything their space offered them and tap into every resource. What they produced was a direct result of using what was available. What an awesome "read the room to win" message!

Cybersecurity sales have a similar "read the room" rule. The first thing you will do when you step into the world of Cybersecurity sales is recognize and familiarize yourself with the environment you are operating from. The approach and strategy you use will depend on the ecosystem and tools surrounding you. If the environment is a siberX conference, small networking event at a basketball game or just lunch, you will need to present in a way that resonates with the ambiance and mood of the event. Your social and outgoing vibe will dominate the sales experience if you are in a social setting. Remember, people buy from people they like. Make sure they see you before seeing what you are selling. Give them a chance to know you and like you.

Trust is at the root of everything we do in Cybersecurity and applies to people, process and technology. We are always establishing trust making it a critical ingredient to the sales process. Establishing trust with your client will pave a path that allows you to showcase how your solution can address their needs. Once the client is sure that you have a solid grasp of their fundamental "problem statement," you will have earned the trust needed to move towards offering solutions. Your ability to recognize their specific problem while providing your offering as the right solution to it will win you the day.

The following are the more common Cybersecurity sales segments with relevant use cases. Here, we will examine how typical cybersecurity companies adopt these sales segments in their strategy:

SALES CHANNELS:
INSIDE AND OUTSIDE SALES

"While cybersecurity sales leaders tend to share some common traits, some have other attributes, which propel/allow them to rise above the crowd."

Daniel Pinsky

1. INSIDE CYBERSECURITY SALES

David Mahdi states, *"In this approach, the inside cybersecurity sales team conducts outreach to prospects, and engages them to buy their cybersecurity solutions. The term 'inside' is a description, in that the team typically consists of sales professionals that conduct their business via methods that aren't face-to-face or onsite. The inside sales team typically doesn't engage in external or outside activities like on-site client visits. Although sometimes, team members might attend industry events where they might staff their booths to demonstrate products and meet with prospects. "*

The team, in most cases, employs sales development representatives (SDRs) and/or automated sales software or tools to identify the needs of prospects and track their journey until sales have been won. Remember, maintaining sharp organization skills, consistently following up with clients and staying hungry are key.

A valuable point here from David is that "One notable advantage of inside sales is that costs are much lower than outside or field sales (i.e. outside sales typically incur costs such as car allowances, fuel mileage, etc.). Costs here are usually base salaries, commissions, equipment/software costs, and related benefits. Inside sales tend to be a great entry point for new and/or aspiring sales professionals. And while many can have long and fruitful careers as inside sales representatives, some see it as a stepping stone to outside or field sales."

2. OUTSIDE CYBERSECURITY SALES

In this approach, much like the inside sales team, the outside cybersecurity sales team conducts outreach to prospects and engages them to buy their cybersecurity solutions. However, their focus is on meeting with clients face to face. This could be on-site at the client's location and/or off-site activities such as meeting over coffee, meals, or industry events.

The primary sales approach occurs outside the office, door-to-door or in what is also known as 'field sales.' Outside sales may be required for specific market segments, clients, and jurisdictions. Often, the target personas for outside sales tend to be the clientele that prefers face-to-face or onsite meetings. Generally speaking, this tends to be aligned to executive sales, for example, when targeting CISOs, CIOs and other CXOs. There also might be cultural drivers for meeting face to face in some countries and jurisdictions. For example, in regions such as Asia, and the Middle East, many clientele might prefer to conduct business face-to-face.

An outside sales representative is constantly on the go. Their office can be wherever a client needs them, whether at a Toronto Maple Leaf's hockey game (still waiting for that Stanley Cup) or at a downtown Thai place that you've never even heard of. A successful outside sales representative can support a range of tasks that require exceptional management and multitasking skills. Handling day-to-day schedules and coordinating calendars with clients, traversing city streets, dealing with public transportation, and the logistics of parking vehicles all require superior time management skills to maintain focus on high impact and priority engagements.

Being able to strategically plan their use of time, have a solid sense of cultural awareness, and be resilient and resourceful are critical skills that every outside sales representative needs. Handling unexpected bumps is all part of an outside sales representative's territory. Suppose a restaurant reservation is accidentally cancelled, and you are left with your decision-maker client waiting. In that case, you will know exactly how to take action and proceed towards the goal gracefully. A successful outside sales representative will have backup plans that can be put into seamless action.

Presentation skills and communication skills must be polished at all times. Dressing appropriately for the occasion (formal vs casual attire) is important. Basic table manners and proper etiquette (yes, there is a right way to eat and drink during meals) are critical elements in an outside sales role. Social etiquette plays a vital role in outside sales.

I asked George Al-Koura to provide some insight; he has this important perspective:

The ability to build, evolve and manage your client relationships from cold opening to year-over-year renewal all comes down to the little details that influence how they 'feel' about you. When so many new products are emerging at such a rate that innovation has become saturated in many industry spaces, the strength of your individual sales relationships will be your biggest differentiators in the eyes of a client who is evaluating competing offers.

With all of that into perspective, outside sales reps tend to have more experience and are generally not a role for those new to sales.

COVID-19 has disrupted the dynamic of outside sales. Some might say it has changed for good while others may see it as a pause. But for some industries and jurisdictions, face-to-face sales are becoming a less adopted approach as we have entered a digital and contactless world. However, when you need to engage every buying team member, it is essential to do so face-to-face or virtually now. This is the oldest and hardest type of selling and makes establishing trust even more critical.

If you watch a sprinter prepare for a 100M dash, they will wear weights on their ankles hours before the race; as soon as the race starts, they take them off, making their feet feel lighter. Once you master outside sales, you can sell in any environment.

THE DYNAMIC OF OUTSIDE AND INSIDE SALES

While some aspiring sales professionals see a sequential career path, where they start in sales development (where the focus is on generating and qualifying leads), then transition to inside sales. Some professionals prefer to remain inside sales. And perhaps this might not make a difference in some market segments, especially due to the COVID-19 pandemic disrupting in-person meetings. As a result of the pandemic, many "outside-sales reps" have transitioned to act like inside sales reps for the bulk of their working hours, as they spend far less time with occasional field visits/activities. Either way, this dynamic will remain a hybrid approach to outside sales for the coming years.

Given the core areas of differentiation and focus for inside and outside sales professionals, there are highly advantageous dynamics when two groups work together to achieve a common goal. That is tag-teaming accounts with an inside/outside blend. Although not all cybersecurity organizations leverage these dynamics, perhaps due to specific market segment needs/barriers, others will leverage the inside sales team to assist outside sales representatives. For example, inside sales representatives could assist outside sales reps by conducting activities such as: calling prospects and clients, booking meetings, and sending quotes and purchase orders. Much of these tasks can be difficult for sales reps in the field. This is highly beneficial to the organization as a whole because outside reps, when in the field, are often occupied by logistical elements (as we discussed above, such as dealing with public transportation, going through airport security, etc.).

MARKETING CHANNELS & TARGET SEGMENTS:

I asked Victoria Vuong, Senior Manager, Strategic Alliances Partner Marketing, Zscaler, whom I have worked with for many years, what happens when you take the power of sales and the innovation and agility of marketing's partnership.

THE POWER OF A TRUE PARTNERSHIP BETWEEN SALES AND MARKETING

I have seen the greatest success in building momentum and driving from goals to objectives to strategy and tactics through Objective Based Marketing. This is key to building a strong Sales and Marketing partnership. It's the ability to put the stake in the ground to say, "this is what I am going to do for your business," based on your goals and objectives – and being able to measure the success and bring back to the business the results to show that marketing has helped move the needle.

As part of the buying journey, more and more people today are self-educating, consuming information, and engaging content in different ways and at their own pace. And as the buyer's journey is not always linear, you can say that the buyer is designing their path. As such, marketing has had to shift its broad-based segmentation approaches to a journey of personalization. Marketing methods, and tactics haven't changed; however, how we message, target, segment, and microsegment have changed. Building that personalized journey comes to life with an account-based focus, an area where Sales and Marketing meet. Sales and Marketing work together strongly when customer challenges and needs can be uncovered through research, the partner ecosystem, existing marketing analytics, and customer relationships. All of this builds the context in helping to curate a unique and personalized buyer's journey. You can begin to work together and map out customer intent and interests by persona and build a marketing campaign that will help put forth the right mix of information at the right time and place through multi-channels available at all levels of an organization. You can even go one step further in leveraging marketing information gathered to help find the customer's pain and help champion build.

Leveraging a prescribed journey can help educate, positively influence, and create preference at all stages of the funnel, define and convert leads to opportunities, and accelerate deals. The power of the Sales and Marketing partnership can be felt through increased customer engagement, generated pipeline and opportunities, increased average deal size and revenue, and ultimately help to create customer loyalty and advocacy.

3. B2B SALES

B2B is a common acronym in sales that means 'business-to-business.' It describes an approach where companies sell their products and services to other businesses and organizations instead of individual users.

B2B deals are usually high-ticket sales as the products determine the buyers' operations. For instance, if your company sells endpoint security software to hospitals, you follow the B2B approach.

4. B2C SALES

B2C means business-to-consumer. This sales approach deals with relationships and sales transactions between your business and individual users. The sales value can be low, and you need more clients to break even. For example, cybersecurity companies selling antivirus products like Kaspersky, Norton Anti-Virus, AVG, Avast, and others use this approach.

5. BUSINESS DEVELOPMENT

Business development ("BD") is a common role in most cybersecurity organizations that focuses on forging partnerships that span technical integrations, commercial bundling and resale opportunities, or a combination of the two. Business development can help the organization increase product capabilities (by partnering with other solutions) and/or accessing new markets, leading to an expansion of overall business.

SALES DEVELOPMENT: A FUNCTION OF SALES AND MARKETING

Sales development focuses on generating and qualifying leads. The person responsible for business development responsibilities is called the sales development representative (SDR). They develop new business ideas, prospect and qualify leads for the company. Once the SDR is done with lead qualification, the inside or outside sales rep converts the lead into an opportunity. Ultimately, the inside / outside sales rep drives the opportunity to a close.

SDRs understand the business drivers, customers, partners, and competitors. This can be the first touchpoint for many prospects. When leveraged accordingly, SDRs and their teams can help generate qualified sales opportunities, allowing inside and outside sales reps to focus their efforts on closing business. A perfect example is Slack (messaging app for businesses), where the BDM manages the sales pipeline on enterprise accounts. They coordinate outreach to different stakeholders in their respective companies. As product experts, their core responsibility is to create demand for Slack's products. The focus of SDRs on qualifying and generating opportunities can enable a predictable and stable sales pipeline. A qualified and predictable deal pipeline is a positive outcome of a well-run SDR team; as such, a good SDR team is desirable for any cybersecurity sales organization.

SDR teams are a great entry point for aspiring sales professionals, where one can acquire the skills and experience to progress to inside and outside sales.

Finally, the SDR team could be a subset of the marketing organization in some organizations. The logic is that marketing runs lead-generating activities (i.e. industry events, webinars, advertising, etc.); therefore, the SDR team would qualify those leads. Depending on the organization, the SDR function could be placed under marketing and/or sales depending on the organization.

6. AGENCY SALES

This form of sales includes lead generation and conversion of new leads to subscribe to an agency's service packages. Clients can either be signed on a retainer or by the project.

7. DIRECT SALES

The direct selling model bypasses the traditional retail environment to sell to prospects/clients/customers. The seller deals directly with the clients, who are often offered commission or incentives for sharing the products with others.

8. SALES CHANNEL

The channel sales strategy involves using partners and third parties—referral partners, affiliate partners, wholesalers, distributors, managed service providers, marketplaces or value-added resellers—to sell your products or services. This is a contrast to a traditional, direct sales strat-

SALES AND MARKETING CHANNELS IN THE CYBERSECURITY INDUSTRY

INSIDE CYBERSECURITY SALES

OUTSIDE CYBERSECURITY SALES

B2B SALES

B2C SALES

BUSINESS DEVELOPMENT

AGENCY SALES

DIRECT SALES

SALES CHANNEL

PROFESSIONAL SERVICES FIRMS

egy in which your company's sales team is solely responsible for selling products to customers.[5]

KEY TAKEAWAY: Pay attention to the environment you are operating from and adopt an approach within the sales process that is aligned to the specificities of the environment.

9. PROFESSIONAL SERVICES FIRMS

Professional Services (PS) firms are constantly adapting to the latest trends in technology and cybersecurity. It is imperative for PS firms to "stay ahead of the game" and to continue to innovate to serve their client base. PS firms invest a lot of time, money and resources building up their marketing strategies for cybersecurity and constantly revising it. They have set up the right combination of the buns, the meat and everything in between. When you compare a PS firm's marketing strategy from one time frame to another, you will notice that it is always different, always adopting. You should build a similar mindset.

"Be adapting, be different; open doors that you thought never existed." Thank you to #thecyberAli for your wisdom on this.

5   Pipedrive. n.d. "What is Channel Sales | Channel Sales Strategy." Pipedrive. Accessed March 26, 2022. https://www.pipedrive.com/en/blog/channel-sales.

CHAPTER THREE

POINTERS ON SELLING INDUSTRIAL CYBER SECURITY

Daniel Ehrenreich,
Industrial Cybersecurity

INTRODUCTION

Selling technology solutions for cyber secured data communication (IT) was never an easy task, because along the long sales cycle, which can spread from weeks to months, the salesperson has to deal professionally with a range of technology experts in the customers' organization. While dealing with IT projects is complicated, it is even more difficult for Operation technology (OT) projects protecting industrial, manufacturing and utility related facilities. Depending on the project-phase when the opportunity is detected – whether it is a tender or purchase from prequalified turnkey integrators – you must be aware that the process is always long, and every case is different. If you start after the tender is published, the chances to win are low unless your product is listed in the top-right Gartner TM quadrant. From the vendor's point of view, to be successful in a significant project, the sales process must also involve specific technical and maintenance experts.

WHICH TECHNOLOGY SOLUTIONS
ARE PREFERRED?

During the interaction with the customer's team, you will meet people who will examine your technology solution and the proposal according to the IAC or the AIC (A-Availability, I-Integrity, C-Confidentiality) Triad. Although not a perfect approach, this can be fine for a project, where the operation safety is not a major concern. However, when you propose a cyber security solution for a chemical, nuclear or gas operated power plant, the situation is different, and your solution must comply with the SRP (Safety-Reliability-Productivity) Triad.

Taking the correct approach is critical as it may help you with differentiating your approach from the competitors' proposal, who due to lack of understanding the safety risks in the industrial process offer solutions matching the AIC or IAC Triad. It means that you must have the needed expertise in your sales team, who understand the industrial process. If you do not have such an expert internally, it is recommended to hire an OT expert, who can assist you when you discuss the technology proposal with the industrial experts of the customer.

WHO ARE DECISION MAKERS
IN THE ORGANIZATION?

Your process may start with the industrial automation experts of the customer, and they involve the IT experts who understand cyber defense technologies. Each phase in the sales process must be optimally tuned to the technology level of the person you deal with. Some may prefer innovative cyber defense while others may prefer buying a proven, standard-based solution with many references. Along that process you might also meet people having different (sometimes not visible) interest such as personal promotion if the project is successful or prior to their retirement, might prefer slowing down the process.

Furthermore, it is important to remember, that when you deal with the top-floor executives, who are the ultimate decision maker for large projects, they are not cyber security experts and want to hear that the proposed solution will assure business continuity for the industrial plant rather than hearing about cyber defense solution. Important to remember that discussing Return on Investment (RoI) is in most cases not applicable for cyber defense.

BENCHMARK YOUR SOLUTION ACCORDING TO SWOT CHARTS

You always need to understand the solutions of your competitors; those who offer end-to-end solution and those who offer just a specific hardware or software for the system. Based on that, you may initiate carefully planned actions to weaken their solution. If applicable to your product, you may raise claims related to compliance with the ISA 62443 standard, sections 4.1 and 4.2 referring to cyber security life cycle management for industrial systems.

If you detected the project at its early stage, it is recommended conducting a project-specific SWOT (Strengths - Weaknesses - Opportunities - Threats) analysis. During that process, put your SWOT quadrant and each of your competitors' SWOT charts with details specifically applicable TO the customer's industrial process and the requested cyber defense architecture side-by-side. Obviously, it cannot be an accurate comparison, if needed and time allows, you may decide on quick actions to close critical gaps.

HOW DO YOU CLOSE THE DEAL AHEAD OF COMPETITORS?

Depending on the urgency of project completion and your readiness with an effective and competitive solution, you may take actions to expedite the decision process or to slow it down. Understanding the most important and valued features, during the discussion with customer's industrial and cyber security experts you may highlight the benefits of your solution versus the weaknesses of your competitors.

If time allows, you may create a non-visible partnership with other vendors and even with some competitors towards creating a specification-compliant solution integrated with your or their proposal. Always remember that there is no single solution which assures absolute cyber defense (no silver bullet) and various solutions can be effective.

SUMMARY AND CONCLUSION

The most crucial factor in the selling process is your ability to listen and understand the specific factors driving the project. Never underestimate the 'people factor' and evaluate how someone might harm your efforts or contribute to the selection of your solution. It involves understanding the goals of the organization and goals of people dealing with vendor selection such as: compliance with regulation, recent cyber incident at a similar facility.

Being aware of these topics, carefully explain to the customer the combined CapEx (acquisition cost) and the OpEx (operation cost) figures as applicable to your solution versus competitors. Finally, always be optimistic, support your customer's view and be patient.

CHAPTER FOUR

THOUGHTS ON GENDER AND SALES

Karen Nemani
Cybersecurity Professional

When it comes to cybersecurity sales you'll find women working at every stage and in every type of role. Women sell cybersecurity products; as consultants women sell cybersecurity services and women are part of the organizational sale chain too - if not at the top, they are somewhere in the decision-making process. Therefore, considering how gender and sales interact can be as important when it comes to selling in cybersecurity – both for salesperson awareness and to close a successful sale.

WOMEN IN CYBERSECURITY SALES

In sales, key performance indicators are straightforward. Meet or exceed your target. Despite this, there are very few women in cybersecurity sales and while there are likely a world of reasons, two main reasons standout: There is a distinct recruitment bias towards hiring men, and women don't get promoted, making it an unattractive career path. Add the 'bro' culture and we start seeing how women don't easily find this a compelling career path. There are also general assumptions about what is needed to succeed in a sales role. "The belief is that you need to be outgoing, an extrovert, or have the 'gift of gab'. However sales isn't about talking or being an extrovert; rather it's about curiosity and bringing your own authentic style."

Women who do get hired find they have to work harder to rationalize the hire and be quick to show their value and worth as salespeople. When they succeed, it is financially rewarding. Yet in order to achieve career success women need access to opportunities, support, along with paths to advancement.

Women don't often get promoted in cybersecurity sales. Those that do, tend to get directed into customer renewals or commercial sales with the underlying, unspoken rationale being those roles don't require as much travel therefore women can be home for their families. There is also the understanding that if a salesperson takes time off, they may lose their territory and trajectory of success as any time off can lead to a failure to meet targets.

Women who are successful, and there ARE women who are successful cybersecurity salespeople, find there is yet another challenge. In building their worth and value as sales people, women who are successful tend to end up so successful they derail their path to advancement into management or becoming a Chief Revenue Officer as high performers are a financial boon to companies. Why would they advance them to another role?

Women in cybersecurity sales share that they find success through their sales style which they see as more authentic and aware. Do we need managers out in the field selling or do we need Sales Management to be inspiring? I would suggest that the answer is we need both and inspiring sales management could easily translate to a leadership and mentorship style that can be shared across an entire sales team creating a team of high performers. Sales is not there yet and currently, women need to maintain a level of effort to prove themselves again and again effectively building a challenging journey that can lead to burnout and cause them to leave.

Any woman selling a cybersecurity product or service starts their journey with some degree of handicap – a hurdle they must overcome. Whether it's believability that they understand the technology or the customer need or more generally, there is often the question as to whether they understand cybersecurity at all. In fact when selling to male executives, more often than not men are selected to deliver the sales pitch and close the sale – even if there is a woman present who is as capable. In this way their sales opportunities can be limited. These historical biases place women working in cybersecurity sales in a position where they need to be creative. It starts with defining their role in the sales cycle. They need to know more and share right away that they are serious, knowledgeable sales people; that they know as much, if not more than their male counterparts. While sales for men often start with understanding the needs and the direction of their customers, women have the added layer of understanding and assessing whether there is inherent bias that will impede the sale and create a strategy to address and overcome those biases without offending the customer.

I've found women who work in cybersecurity sales often start off their sales conversation by showcasing their knowledge with a focus on proving they know what they are talking about so that customers are willing to listen. This creates an extra hurdle they face in their sales process – the act of confirming their legitimacy as cybersecurity salespeople. It's not the only one though.

Imagine this, a female cybersecurity saleswoman is at a conference at her company's booth and standing next to her is a 'sales model' (usually female) who's been invited there by the company who believe that sales needs 'pretty women' as window dressing to draw customers to their booth. Now if you're male and reading this, take a moment and picture yourself talking to a CISO while standing beside a male model (dress him in a Speedo to really get the idea) and consider how you would sell in that situation. Many women in cybersecurity sales have worked in similar type situations and while the approach may draw in some customers, the focus is already redirected away from the product they want to sell. Also, as a female purchaser, I can assure you the underlying message has the opposite effect. Overall it creates a challenge for women selling in cybersecurity as they are expected to smile and sell while standing next to another woman there for a completely different purpose – one that effectively undermines their legitimacy and ability to sell. These are hurdles that can make closing the deal for women selling in cybersecurity all the more challenging. Yet despite these challenges, women who sell in the cybersecurity space are out there every day superbly navigating these roadblocks and succeeding.

SELLING TO WOMEN

The majority of the discussion on cybersecurity sales leverages a model based on understanding a fair bit of information about the target customer from knowing the needs and goals, regulatory commitments, past organizational performance (i.e. breaches), and of course, current and future projects. Knowing who the customer is, is also incredibly important and if the customer is a woman, I propose adding to the above list a self-awareness and self-bias check. What does this mean? It means salespeople – men and women - might want to consider whether their approach would engage a female cybersecurity practitioner and determine whether there is gender bias at play. If it is and you don't know it, know that the sale likely is gone before you even start the conversation.

Checking your gender bias comes in many forms from assessing the language you use to the type of approach you take. It should include practicing with women in the field, your female colleagues and being prepared to get a little uncomfortable because you likely have norms that are inappropriate and you might not know it. Then try changing it up - at conferences, on calls and elsewhere, and be open to self checks and feedback that will help you reframe your bias if it's in play. Know that if you're mid-conversation and you notice the attention turn elsewhere, your calls repeatedly get ignored after what you thought was a successful first contact or they simply walk away, there might be gender bias at play and therefore there's an issue with your approach and delivery. I invite cybersecurity salespeople – both men and women - to consider the following: Take a moment to think about the language you plan on using. Consider the tactics you deploy – they may work fine for some men but may well make women uncomfortable (i.e. trust me, it's a sexy solution and will work!). Ensure there is respect and awareness in the conversation.

There are many stories – mine included – where a woman gets a call based on their title yet the salesperson starts the conversation by asking who is 'the right person' to talk to about cybersecurity. One security conference I attended had a vendor product I was quite excited to see in action and ask questions about. So I did. The salesperson was very nice. After introducing himself, he asked me where I worked and once I shared, he proceeded to name a number of men at my organization – in fact a couple of them worked for me - then suggested I go speak with them so I could understand how the product could be of benefit to our organization. Apparently he did not have the time to answer my questions yet when the person beside me (a male) asked some of the same questions I did, he began explaining in detail. Don't forget that salespeople are often the initial face of your organization and it matters who is speaking for you. I can say that I won't forget that person, the product or the company and though a good product, it took some time before the company showed a shift in their culture and approach through their sales people.

Another bias that comes into play when selling cybersecurity products or services to women is this ongoing assumption that women are 'not technical' and only have 'soft skills' to contribute alongside a basic cybersecurity understanding. While this is a sweeping generalization that could apply to any human working in cybersecurity, it's incredibly prevalent when it comes to discussing and selling cybersecurity products and services with women in the field. I cannot tell you how many times a salesperson starts off with a security primer or patronizingly introduces negativity into the conversation with the assumption that I do not understand what they are talking about when discussing technical aspects of cybersecurity.

These are but a couple of examples that highlight an underlying bias that reinforces negative messages for women working in cybersecurity– messages that our value lies in our ability to connect salespeople to someone important – someone with decision-making authority – and that would not be us. Messages that we cannot possibly understand technical capabilities and solutions. Know that these messages are biases and they shut down potentially fruitful sales avenues. The suggestion in this book, to know your customer/client should include a knowledge and awareness of your inherent assumptions and biases – including gender. Add in questioning your personal bias with a view to shifting your approach (to throw them away) and reframing it based on your awareness.

WOMEN SELLING CYBERSECURITY SERVICES

Female cybersecurity consultants and practitioners have slightly different hurdles to navigate. Cybersecurity has grown incredibly competitive. There's an ongoing practice among practitioners who feel the need to introduce themselves and share what I call their 'cyber-pedigree' right away – as if we all need to prove our worthiness to be considered a cybersecurity practitioner in the field. Now imagine adding gender to this conversation. With so few women working in the field and many leaving, the proof women need to show is more often subject to skepticism and disbelief. Alternatively there is the belief that they are in their role solely for the purpose of diversity and inclusion. As a result, women's expertise and experience gets devalued and questioned. The perceived sensitivity of women means we are questioned as to whether we can make tough decisions or navigate difficult people; whether we truly understand the technology (despite having worked with it before); or whether we have the ability to navigate tough situations and be alright with being the only woman in the room. Through both my own experience and the women in cybersecurity whom I've had the privilege of working with, I've observed the following attributes: When we say we know something, we do. Know that we are well aware we get questions and often study many times longer and know more than we need to as we're often called upon to prove it. Even then we are faced with disbelief. When asked if we can navigate difficult people and make tough decisions know that working in this field for more than one year alone builds a repertoire of skills and expertise that go beyond cybersecurity. In fact, we navigate difficult conversations and resistance with mostly every step we take. Not many men face these hurdles and while a challenge, the experience women have navigating our cybersecurity careers will serve any organization in good stead. In fact I'd go as far as to suggest even better. As for selling our cybersecurity services? Hire us. Watch us. We can and have delivered secure cybersecurity programs and exceptionally well too. Many say women have a confidence issue. I disagree and propose we consider it is a perception issue.

One way to consider the above is to add a positive bias to your gendered understanding. Consider that women are socialized to navigate risk and security from the moment we are born. We are taught that we are not secure and are responsible for maintaining our personal security. We are expected to manage risk every time we step out of our homes alone. It has long been our responsibility to see to our own safety and to our children's safety. Interestingly, we might want to consider that socialization of women makes us more suited to managing and delivering cybersecurity including selling it as we've been trained to identify risk and socialized with the mindset needed to effectively manage those risks at every turn. The fact that the world looks at it otherwise is based on a rhetoric that gets reinforced through the language of cybersecurity; when we talk about women bringing 'soft skills' to cybersecurity, and the perception that women don't have technical skills. Women bring multiple skills to the table and technical skills are one of many – as are the ability to communicate, manage risk and protect assets. While this is a book in and of itself, overall, it is a perception issue – one that has grown and frames gender in such a way as to undermine women's ability to be considered as legitimate and worthy cybersecurity practitioners that are necessary in every cybersecurity team.

CHAPTER FIVE

ENGAGING THE ENTERPRISE CUSTOMER

Hashim Hussein
Cybersecurity Sales Professional

In Sales, there are different ways of selling from small vs large customers, and this could be based on revenue or the number of employees. In this section, we will focus on selling into a large enterprise and the process of driving the sale to close. Enterprise sales reps know the fundamentals of sales, the competition, technology, the vertical and the customer use cases before they target the prospect. Complexity is common when dealing with enterprise clients such as banks, insurance companies, healthcare institutions, and government agencies. Enterprise reps must possess key attributes such as patience, attention to detail, and a strategic mindset. A strategic mindset can hone in on tactical activities such as aligning internal resources and orchestrating the multiple steps needed to validate the deal and when it will close (i.e forecasting).

The average sales cycle with an Enterprise client can range from 12-48 months, depending on the technology being sold. The baseline is understanding the customer challenges and making sure the solution you are selling solves a business problem and has an ROI/TCO metric aligned right of the gates. The conversation can start at the CIO or CISO level to ensure the solution is a fit and a budget can be allocated. If it's a start-up technology, start with a director or the technical team to validate the solution, solve some of their technical needs, and then go to the CIO or CISO.

The art of selling starts once the cybersecurity sales representative completes the validation process. The Sales Engineer (SE) will kick off a Proof of Concept (POC) with the customer technical team, which could be from 15 to 20 people depending on the size of the customer. This is a critical process in the sale cycle and has multiple steps. For example, aligning a project manager for the POC to ensure the client and the vendor will deliver results in 30, 60 or 90 days, designing a current state and future state architecture etc. In short, the goal is to make sure the technology works, solves the business problem and gets a technical win from the customer.

In parallel, Enterprise sales reps pay attention to detail and are a few steps ahead of the customer. Top reps start working with the business to ensure the following: NDA is signed, draft Statement of Work (SOW) is ready, ensuring Privacy concerns are addressed, Compliance like ISO and SOC 2 have been validated by the customer Risk team, helping the customer build a business case that includes financials, competitive landscape on why they chose your technology, use case solved, results from the POC are all part of working the deal.

There are some tough questions the sales rep can ask:

- Who is going to deploy the solution?

- How is it going to be managed once deployed?

- Do you have a resource that will own and manage this technology going forward?

- How many people on the team will invest in getting certified on the platform?

This is what differentiates the Enterprise sales rep. They have prepped the customer to present to their board with all the metrics and data points covered, ensuring the project is approved and ready to be executed.

The last stage is working with the procurement team. If it's a government client, make sure contracts are aligned to execute. Most Enterprise customers will write an RFP.

The cybersecurity sales representative must have a relationship with the author of the RFP to provide all the information to help them win the deal. Another critical step for the sales rep is to get the legal team to review the software/hardware vendor contract. Missing this step can cause a significant delay to the purchase.

CHAPTER SIX

ENGAGING THE CHIEF INFORMATION SECURITY OFFICER OR SELLING TO CISO

"Most CISOs know they can't do everything by themselves. They need an ecosystem team to have visibility around the world. The Good CISOs have a very good network of partners, vendors, service providers, industry peers, law enforcement, not just their direct reports."

Abbas Kudrati

Abbas Kudrati, award-winning CISO, cloud & cybersecurity strategist, professor of practice, executive advisory board member, author, thought leader, keynote speaker and director and chief cybersecurity advisor for Microsoft has some great advice on selling to a CISO.

The role of the security department (and CISO) can vary widely; the variety of security department charters will impact what decisions and processes security will be involved in your overall sales cycle. This can change with the leadership qualities of the CISO and the willingness/culture of the business to accept a change in security's role.

A typical track is for the part of the CISO and security organization to progress in power and maturity to the right and increase ownership/responsibility for technical matters. The most significant shift in the maturity of security's role within the organization is when security/CISO develops business skills and relationships. This is massively different from the technical orientation mindset on the right; the business orientation is focused on developing relationships with the business to understand their needs, ambitions, initiatives, and other risks that should be balanced against security risks.

Note: If the CISO is business/strategic oriented, they typically heavily influence approving/blocking initiatives (dependent on where they are vs. CIO in the organization chart). Learn how security fits in your customer's culture! If security culture is weak, Business and IT stakeholders will see security as a cost to minimize/avoid.

UNDERSTAND YOUR CUSTOMER REALITIES

- **BUSINESS/ORGANIZATIONAL LEADERS:**

  » Business downtime and cost

  » Own both organizational risk and opportunity

- **CISO & SECURITY ORGANIZATION:**

  » Translate security risk into business risk

  » Security risk expertise and operations

- **CIO & IT ORGANIZATION:**

  » Secure IT solutions and operations

  » Attacks damage IT availability and uptime

Before you go and engage with an Organization's CISO, let us understand the CISO's role in detail.

UNDERSTANDING THE CISO ROLE

The CISO is responsible for overall information security, risk and compliance and all aspects related to cyber security tools. The CISO oversees and directs security programs across the organization to ensure information assets are adequately protected. The CISO provides vision and leadership for initiatives ensuring alignment with business goals and risk thresholds.

ROLE EVALUATION

CISO's role is broadening from IT security-focused to encompassing risk management responsibilities. A CISO needs to understand IT, OT and the business increasingly. There is much ongoing discussion about where the CISO should sit within the organization. It's key to understand company culture and organization to ensure the CISO reports to the leader who manages risk.

KEY RESPONSIBILITY

- Lead security executive steering committees and panels, ensuring that various stakeholders' expectations are met.

- Establish external relationships with regulatory, public, and industry organizations (law enforcement, government agencies, etc.). Capitalize on strong ties with consulting and technology firms to maximize value and security investment efficiency.

- Establish a robust security initiative management lifecycle for different delivery practices (preparation, assessment, planning, execution, & measuring).

- Structure security spending budgets, resource allocation, investment prioritization, overall effectiveness and efficiency of security capabilities.

- Influence tool selection based on best practices, legal drivers, compliance drivers and industry standards.

ROLE (CISO) CHALLENGES

- Abiding by changing law and compliance regulations that are becoming increasingly complex

- Making sure security has a seat at the table for the strategic initiatives of the company to ensure they have a line of sight and are involved in the planning strategy of the company.

- Security is often looped in after the fact, rather than earlier in the design phase. Suppose things are built by the technology side alone. In that case, systems tend to focus more on speed and agility than on security

- Ensuring that they have the bases covered as best they can with as much scale and proactive insight as possible to cover changing threat landscapes

- Inadequate alignment with lines of business and being seen as blockers versus enablers

REPORTING STRUCTURE

- While most commonly reporting to the CIO, the CIO generally has dotted line responsibilities to several other C-suite leaders, both as an advisor on information security and as a way to create independence from the IT organization

- Reporting structure can vary based on industry and size of the company

  » Compliance-focused and regulated industries may have the CISO reporting to the Chief Financial Officer (CFO) or General Counsel

- The recent shift to reporting to the Chief Risk Officer (CRO). Regulators view that as a positive because it separates security from technology, so the two don't compete for the same dollars

- Reporting to the CRO can also improve the CISO's understanding of cybersecurity and its relationship to overall risk

TOOLS AND TECHNOLOGY DESCRIPTION

CISOs empower their direct reports/line of businesses to make tool decisions following strategic roadmaps and security architecture design. Though not the owner of specific tools, CISOs provide budget, influence, and final sign-off of security tool purchases. CISOs are more interested in platforms versus point solutions.

Buying all the point solutions means more money and integration and creates many management issues. The ability to expand the capabilities of existing tools and technologies will minimize the required investment.

Most sought-after features for the technology solutions needed:

- Integrated dashboards with complete upstream visibility (security, risk and compliance) without being fragmented across various platforms

- Board-level reporting

- Strong access of control of people and things

- Agile risk management capabilities

- Consolidated view of threat feeds/intelligence sources

DO'S AND DON'TS FOR SELLING TO CISOS

No two CISOs are the same:

- They come from different personalities, different backgrounds (technology, finance, risk/legal, etc.), different businesses/industries and different risks.

Listen first and act (sell) later:

- Always try to listen and learn about their specific risks and concerns they may have specific to their organization and industry.

- Always focus on their problems and never lead with 'asking for approval' or budget.

- First things first - Many of your products or services may help, but it's critical to start with the most important stuff; otherwise, it may be seen as "hard selling."

Be confident but don't fake it:

- Be confident, but don't pretend to be the expert if you're not.

- Never promise that you or your product/service offering will 100% solve anything.

- Last but not least, say, "I don't know" when you don't. You will be more respected in this case.

CHAPTER SEVEN

HOW TO BECOME GREAT
AT CYBERSECURITY SALES

"Be optimistic and you will be successful."

Ali ibn Abi Talib

I have always loved sports. If I were not writing this book right now, you would probably find me playing basketball or watching the game. It isn't really about the actual sport itself that gets me hooked. The players' integrity keeps me in a constant state of awe. Have you ever wondered why fans get so emotional when the team's superstar misses a key move? It's because the fans know what every player is capable of. We understand and can see when a player performs at their level best. We can see excellence. Whether it's Michael Jordan, Tiger Woods, Serena Williams, Wayne Gretzky or Mohammad Ali, the greatness within them was the unwavering commitment to the development of themself.

I firmly believe that doing your best to be your best is excellence. To be your best, you have to know yourself and master the art of being you. It's important to understand all aspects of you, we all have different shadings to us, some dark some light. Shining the light on those darker areas and focusing on that side helps to highlight the qualities that are within yourself. Within that, honour yourself and serve your purpose.

As with any sport, indisputable distinct characteristics make a winner a winner. Cybersecurity sales leaders are the same. The good news is that these traits can be learned and mastered. It is a mission that is 100% possible.

So my friends, your mission, should you choose to accept it, is to read the following eight-to-great commandments, memorize them, understand them, apply them, and master them.

Unlike the missions given to Ethan Hunt (Tom Cruise) in every Mission Impossible movie, this book will not self-destruct, so read it once, twice, or as many times as you need, to embrace all that it offers.

1. THOU SHALL: ALWAYS STAY COMPOSED

"In the midst of movement and chaos, keep stillness inside you."
Deepak Chopra

It's 1:37 a.m., and you can't sleep. You toss and turn for a while until finally, you surrender yourself into the cell phone placed within arms reach, sitting on your nightstand, next to your ChapStick because nobody wants chapped lips at night.

You know that you should have listened to your better half and left all of your gadgets downstairs, but you can't seem to not bring your cell phone to bed with you. It's a trap you set for yourself, and now, you are about to walk into that trap all by yourself for the next hour of non-sleeping mindlessness.

As you scroll down your favourite YouTube alley, you land on one of those videos showing how crazy people can be. The story is always the same and always leaves you with second-hand embarrassment for the star of the spectacle. It's a person freaking out at another person because of something that didn't meet their expectation or need. The person freaking out is entirely out of control, they have no idea that someone is recording them, and as a result, they will be tomorrow's viral sensation being featured in the crazy category. Whether it's a fight over a parking spot or a refund that cannot be issued, the lack of composure in the conduct demonstrated is screaming for help. Though you cannot help from the comfort of your bed, you do appreciate that the video helped you get your sleepy sensation back. It's now 2:43 a.m., and you manage to fall asleep.

In Cybersecurity, a sales representative who cannot maintain composure during the various conundrums that pop up can also hurt one's brain! And so, my friends, it is crucial that you master control of your emotions.

Having the ability to respond intellectually instead of emotionally reacting is what lights the way through every single challenge. As a cybersecurity sales representative, your customer will throw unexpected requests and objections at you. Being sensible and pragmatic in your approach will determine how the rest of that interaction plays out. The quality of the interaction and relationship between yourself and your client is dependent on your ability to stay as cool as a cat and as calm as a clam. Patience is a virtue, and it is also your saviour in sales.

Sales result from a successful conversation, and a great conversation results from listening. Learn to listen so that you can improve your understanding. Once you understand, offer a response that adds value to the client's perspective – not yours.

Remember, it is the client's statements that allow you to probe further and obtain additional information to correlate solutions appropriately. Let's assume your client requests a security product's trial extension. Instead of responding with an impulsive "perfect, we can do that!", consider one of the following options:

1. I would love to understand how your experience has been and what you wish you had a chance to explore further.

2. I understand that as our product certainly is vast. May I ask what you feel is missing in terms of your experience during the trial period you had?

You won't always hit the ground running, and it's not always easy to think quickly on your feet. There will be times when you cannot articulate the best open-ended questions during a conversation with a client. However, it can be an artfully acquired skill with practice and commitment. Being prepared with backup responses that allow for more time is a great way to manage expectations while offering practical solutions. A simple "let me look into the trial extension and get back to you" can give you the space you need to create your plan of action.

KEY TAKEAWAY: Practice using effective open-ended questions. Keep it simple and use the same ones every time. This helps to ensure consistency in your approach and mastery of your skill. As with any relationship and interaction, projecting negative emotion or aggression will result in a loss of respect and the opportunity to build a relationship and close a deal. You will not close every time, but you will learn 100% of the time with the right mindset. Do not compromise your composure; not now and not ever.

2. THOU SHALL: DROP THE EGO

"I've missed more than 9,000 shots in my career. I've lost almost 300 games. Twenty-six times I've been trusted to take the game-winning shot and missed. I've failed over and over and over again in my life. And that is why I succeed." — Michael Jordan

If I could implore you to do one thing that will help you in every chapter of your life, it would be to commit to learning about yourself. When you have a free weekend, visit your favourite bookstore, and buy a few books that can help you learn about human nature and the psychology of being human. You will find that through this journey, the more you know about human behaviour, the more you will know about yourself, and the more that you know about yourself, the more you will know about the world.

I have always been fascinated by human behaviour. What makes people do the things that they do? What happened to them that influenced whom they became? There is wisdom in the contemplation of this very intriguing subject.

Part of being human is understanding the impact of our ego. We all have an ego, and it is mostly a good thing. However, when inflamed or bruised, an unchecked ego can move from the essential healthy dose of narcissism (that gifts us with our self-worth and confidence) towards toxic narcissistic energy that holds us back from everything and anything good for us.

How one responds to threats targeting the ego results from many things. To name a few, our unique life experiences, exposure to traumatic events, quality of education, and clarity in the awareness of our whole self all directly impact whom we become.

There is a fine balance between confidence and self-consciousness related to a healthy egoic state and our topic of sales. On the one hand, you need to have the confidence and belief that you can win. On the flip side, you need to understand that you will not always win. There will be times that you fail. This does not make you a failure. It makes you human. Being able to fall gracefully and rise with a collection of inner wisdom and life lessons is the best way to nurture and honour your healthy egoic self. Using self-consciousness as a scapegoat not to succeed can become a self-fulfilling prophecy. Approach every obstacle from a "what is this moment teaching me" perspective and keep everything that does not serve you away from your true self. Anytime you hear your negative inner thoughts, shut it up. Do not let it manifest anywhere. If you protect your thoughts, they will serve you well. All it takes is a bit of self-awareness.

Remember, even the great Michael Jordan understood that there was always something he could improve on and learn. He did that because he knew he had a responsibility to participate in his journey towards excellence. He believed he was worthy and chose not to drown in self-pity whenever he missed the mark. This earned him the legendary status that he has today and will always have.

So my friends, understand that though you are not perfect, you are very deserving. When a client rejects you, fall with grace. Pick up the lessons and rise like the resilient phoenix that you are.

3. THOU SHALL: MAKE EVERY MINUTE COUNT

"An inch of time is an inch of gold, but you can't buy time with an inch of gold." — Chinese Proverb

Though I do not consider myself an official globe-trotter, I am grateful for my travels. I've been fortunate to have visited over twenty countries to date.

From the breathtakingly beautiful beaches of Colombia to the vibrant street culture of Goa, and from the delicate precision of the pastries in France to the loving hospitality offered in Jamaica, all of my travel experiences have had one thing in common: Journeying through airports and airlines.

I learned that the quality of my commute improved significantly through proper planning and due diligence. I made it a point to learn about the airports I would be visiting. What can I eat? Where can I rest? What is there to do and explore at the airport? Planning all of these details became just as important as packing for the trip itself.

I even tried to learn a few sentences in the country's primary language because I do love meeting new people, and hey, if my terrible

Spanish can add a funny ice-breaker with a stranger in Colombia, and entertain me during a flight delay, then learning a bit of Spanish is well worth the effort!

Before my departure date, I took the time to understand everything I could to elevate my entire experience. My time has always been and will always be something I value as priceless. Making sure the time I have serves my purpose is pure joy.

As a sales representative, mastering the use of every minute is as rewarding as the win itself.

A successful cybersecurity sales rep will spend 80% of their time researching everything there is to know about the client and spend 20% of their time on the field.

When travelling, I make it a point to check in online and do whatever else I can do in advance to maximize my time at an airport. Similarly, a top-performing cybersecurity sales rep will find a way to automate repetitive and redundant tasks to save their valuable time and use it towards what matters. They focus on what the goal is, which is closing deals. Using any resources available to maximize efficiency is part of the due diligence you owe to yourself. Find a CRM, Software or a process that works and allow yourself to experience the joy of exploring the sale without getting stuck in the small stuff. All leaders have an efficient and effective process that works for them.

Take the time to understand what works for you and what honours the time you have. Respect the integrity of your journey.

4. THOU SHALL: BE CONFIDENT

"Nothing can dim the light that shines from within." Maya Angelou

I was fourteen years old when I got my first job. I would sell garbage bags to prospective clients. I earned about $50 a month and a lot of belief in myself. I spent every last dollar on candy, and man, was it a sweet victory!

For a high school freshman, $50 a month was pretty awesome in those days. Earning that money gave me an edge, and my desire to maximize my potential grew with that edge. If I could go from not knowing anything about selling, much less selling garbage bags, to earning myself a monthly candy fund, what else could I achieve?

HOW TO BECOME GREAT AT CYBERSECURITY SALES

ALWAYS STAY COMPOSED

DROP THE EGO

THEY MAKE THEIR TIME COUNT

THEY ARE CONFIDENT

THEY ARE LIFELONG LEARNERS

THEY ARE PERSISTENT YET POLITE

THEY ARE TECH-SAVVY

THEY ARE THE REAL DEAL

I committed myself to master my craft. I decided to use different approaches with my customers and practiced various sales and closing strategies. I failed many times, but I also used the lessons to modify my pitch until I found the right one.

I can honestly say that my confidence back then enabled me to establish the foundation that would later lead me to write a book teaching the art of selling.

Being successful in cybersecurity sales requires confidence and the ability to push yourself to face challenges and enjoy the journey through them. Understanding customer problems and industry challenges and creating strategies that can sell the security products' features, functionality, and use cases are all part of your craft.

Top cybersecurity sales leaders innovate themselves on changes in best practices, guidelines, standards, and rules that govern their industry.

Mastering the art of selling cybersecurity begins with confidence. When done well, not only do you end up winning with sales, but you become industry experts and trusted advisors. A successful cybersecurity sales representative can teach their prospects how their businesses operate, from daily processes to industry practices.

As a result, a successful cybersecurity sales representative develops a natural advantage that will forever be valuable to the companies they establish relationships with. Aside from teaching clients about their products, they can provide guidance related to different aspects of their business. At present, people might want to depend on Google Assistant, Alexa, or Siri for basic information, which means sales leaders need to offer unique value and take a consultant position.

It's a paradox, but the best cybersecurity sales professionals focus on disqualifying deals, rather than qualifying. Don't burn cycles on clients that aren't ready to buy, or don't meet qualification guidelines. They need to earn your time too! The focus on disqualifying will help you to focus on high-quality opportunities.

5. THOU SHALL: BE A LIFELONG LEARNER

"Once you stop learning, you start dying." — *Albert Einstein.*

It was a Friday afternoon. I conducted endless interviews to fill a telephone sales consultant role. I remember walking into one specific interview as if it were yesterday.

The candidate sitting across from me had one of the most fascinating answers to a question I had often asked. Why do you want this job? I modified it a bit to understand why the man felt that this was the right role for him in his life, as he was of retirement age.

To this day, the message in his bold response still resonates. He said:

> *Well, I believe that the soul knows what it needs to do to elevate you and prepare you for what is ahead. At this point in my life, when I could be enjoying my retirement, I hear my future self calling me and to get there, I need to do what I think I cannot do. I never thought I could convince someone to purchase an item without my physical presence, and it is for that very reason that I am here. To teach me that the limitation I impose on myself through an unproven thought can be a pathway to something more. I have had a wonderful life, and I want to continue on that path. What has been my greatest joy is allowing all around me to teach me, and I believe that employment here is meant to be a classroom for all that I have yet to know.*

As you can imagine, I was intrigued, amazed and inspired (and yes, pleasantly flabbergasted). I had heard the perfect answers to the typical interview questions that I would often ask, but I had never felt the passion in this form of authentic energy before. Needless to say, he did get the job, met his sales quota, and achieved personal satisfaction in committing to his self-development.

Recognize that your training and education do not end when you meet a set target. Don't let your quota limit your potential. To learn and grow is to live. Now, I am not telling you to stay enrolled in training courses forever. I mean, pay close attention to what everything you experience in life is trying to teach you. Behind every successful cybersecurity salesperson is a relentless focus on exploring new frontiers and learning new things.

It's impossible to advance in your career if you do not prioritize personal development. Cybersecurity sales are constantly evolving, and you have to evolve to survive and thrive continually. A sales technique that worked ten years ago may not work today. It was not normal to have a business meeting through virtual meeting rooms, such as Zoom, ten years ago. Nobody knew COVID-19 was going to lock the world down. The pandemic disrupted the cybersecurity outside sales approach and popularized the inside cybersecurity sales strategy. If you cannot adapt your pace to the changing trends, you may find it challenging to understand your prospects' language. The only thing constant is change. Kush Sharma has some great advice:

If you plan to sell cybersecurity services, strongly consider educating yourself on the security domain you are trying to sell (e.g., application security). Join industry associations, take courses and training, read books/articles, subscribe to mailing lists and network with industry domain SMEs. This will increase your confidence level when interacting with technical cybersecurity clients and give you credibility, thereby building immediate trust.

Embrace every opportunity to obtain more knowledge and skills. After all, you are your greatest project!

6. THOU SHALL: BE PERSISTENT & POLITE

"Energy and persistence conquer all things." — *Benjamin Franklin.*

"Keep going; you got this!"

"Activate your core!"

"Check your form!"

"Exhale, don't hold your breath!"

"3 more, and 2, almost there, last one!"

These are only a few lyrics every personal fitness trainer sings during a strenuous one-hour workout. I know firsthand because I survived the blissful addiction to this beautiful torture. The job of a personal fitness trainer is not to get you to your goal; it is to ensure you know you have it in you to get to that goal. They help you nurture your ability through conscious connection and help you not to pop a kneecap.

There is a certain "je ne sais quoi" or silent-loud-energy that sparkles during a workout session. If you've ever experienced it, you most probably have craved it.

Though several components make a solid workout magical, the most important part of your workout is the persistence you bring to each session. Regardless of how difficult, the ability to not give up is what takes you to your fitness goal. It is a known fact that the last few reps during strength training are the hardest to get through, and it is no surprise that those few reps (from 9 to 12) are where the magic is found, leading to transformation. You've seen the regulars at the gym hustling and staying committed to finishing their deadlift sets, regardless of how heavy it is or how tired they are. You may have even seen someone working on their fitness goals through sprinting intervals on the treadmill. You can feel the breathlessness and visualize the silent destination that you imagine them to have in their mind. You can see the sweat and pain on their faces, but that only reinforces their passionate mindset: keep going; no pain, no pleasure! Similarly, persistence during the sales process is an integral part of success.

Over 50% of regular sales reps will abandon prospects after a single follow-up. However, multiple follow-ups are required to convert leads into sales. Persistence is an attribute that allows top cybersecurity salespeople to earn and maintain their "top salesperson" status.

Now, let's be clear on one thing, persistence does not mean stalking. Being charismatic and strategic is important. Your form during barbell squats and the finesse you bring to the workout is just as important as performing. If you call a prospect frequently, it can get to a stage where just seeing your name on caller identification becomes annoying. You do not want to be associated with anything annoying. Following up is only effective when it culminates in a relationship. When you follow up, don't force-feed your products down their throats. Be personable and invite your clients into your energy. Make your presence valuable by making it your mission to add value to their lives through your solution-oriented charm. To achieve what you need to achieve, understand that being polite is a vibe that extends beyond basic pleasantries and manners.

As cliché as it can sound, you need to be a goal-getter. To be your best, you need to be cognizant of the goals you have the power to create. This provides you with the ladder of accountability you need for your progress checks. When you have goals, you have a way to check yourself often. Top salespeople have activity goals, personal goals, stretch goals, and financial goals.

What's even more is that they look beyond quotas. The goals are simply to tell them what they need to go beyond. You grow through your goals, and your goals grow to serve your personal and professional evolution.

7. THOU SHALL: BE TECH-SAVVY

"Technology is just a tool. In terms of getting the kids working together and motivating them, the teacher is the most important." Bill Gates

By now, you probably know that I lived through the beat of the 80s. Here's a secret confession: at times, I am still living in the 80s, and it is epic. Now that we've established that, here's a retro rewind.

It's 1985. You just poured your favourite sugar-filled colourful cereal and spilled milk on the counter again, but that does not slow you down – not even one bit. There are exactly three minutes left until Thundercats, followed by He-Man, air on television. You just finished watching Transformers, and you now reaffirm that you are more than what meets the eye; you are a robot of excellence disguised as a seven-year-old boy in mismatched pj's topped with Saturday morning bedhead hair.

You barely understand the complexities within the ingredients listed on the side of the cereal box, but that doesn't mean anything as it relates to your intellect. What matters most to you at that moment is the successful operation of your television and, of course, the accessories that accompany it. This is what defines the whimsical wisdom in your Saturday morning. You are winning at life, and as long as your sister stays asleep and far away from the threat of taking over the one television in the house to watch She-Ra and Jem and the Holograms, you will continue winning at life.

There is a particular curiosity that children have when it comes to technology. I have yet to meet a toddler who does not know how to operate a cell phone or an iPad. They can't read, but that does not stop them from getting to their favourite YouTube channel, where they are cradled with nonstop lullabies and nursery rhymes. Curiosity creates brilliance!

Being tech-savvy is one of the ongoing shadows that silently creates ease in every aspect of life. For a salesperson, being tech-savvy is also like insurance. For example, anything can go wrong while presenting slides or hosting a virtual meeting; a tech-savvy salesperson would be able to overcome the challenges with ease and complete their presentation.

Cybersecurity salespeople need to know how to troubleshoot common tech issues, optimize internet connections, and unfreeze frozen screens. Having the desire to be efficient is powerful. You can liaise with your IT team to learn how to troubleshoot and optimize technical presentations. The impact is rewarding! A superstar salesperson can demonstrate the ability to demystify complex technical terms in the language that their prospects will understand. Using technology and presenting technology is one way to build trust with your client as someone who can be counted on.

As the world continues to evolve, the one certainty that we can be sure of is that technology is what will lead the way. It always has, and it always will. Taking time to develop your technical aptitude is a not-so-secret ingredient for achieving sustainability and excellence.

8. THOU SHALL: BE THE REAL DEAL

"Know thyself." — Socrates

Authenticity is the loudest energy in any room. You can tell when someone is not thinking their thoughts, speaking in their own words, and being present through their skin. Being your authentic self can be daunting, especially when battling silent insecurities. If you can learn to embrace the weirdness within you, you might just find what distinguishes you from everyone and anything else. The discovery of that is a glorious gift you give to yourself every day.

Accepting all you are and strategically utilizing all those unused parts within you is not taught in school or at work. It is something you practice every day through the power of thought, placement of those thoughts, and the action that follows.

Being the 'real deal' in sales is just as important. Learn how to be you, and you can learn anything. How do you learn how to be you? There is no 'single answer,' but I believe that one of the most powerful teachers is the voice within you. What do your thoughts tell you about yourself? Have you ever listened? Do you know how to listen? Do you even know who you are within yourself? Who is the' your' and who is the 'self' when you approach the concept of yourself in itself?

Every great philosopher, be it Thich Nhat Hanh, Deepak Chopra, Eckhart Tolle, Socrates, or Epictetus (to name a few), has taught that the essence of who you truly are is beyond thought. The premise of mindfulness is the awareness of thought and recognizing power over those thoughts.

Through this awareness, your authentic self surfaces and is fiercely empowered. When you live authentically, the quality in which you do everything is elevated naturally. The control over the thoughts you decide to accept and what thoughts you choose to let go of becomes as natural and innate as the act of breathing is in itself.

The thing about thoughts is that most are based on the external content we are exposed to and consume unconsciously. For example, being over-exposed to the perfect lives captured on our favourite social media influencers online may cause one to think that they live a boring and insignificant life. Although that is untrue, the power of thought can manipulate our identity. Our thoughts convince us to believe that we are defined by the content we consume. We become reduced to the content in and around our lives through that. Whether it is content we experience directly through the journey of our life or the content we absorb based on the lives of others. Either way, the external content is absorbed as a thought, and that thought, when left unaware, can become a toxic reminder that we are not good enough and be good enough; we have to be someone or something else. The birth of insecurities follows, and an internal battle of *you vs. you* ensues. You lose yourself. And now you are not you anymore.

Understand that the realness within you is void of what is external. Create a little bit of space between your thoughts and your power to accept or dismiss your thoughts.

Take a seat in this space. Through this space, you will be able to master the art of mindfulness and maintain authenticity. Better yet, attend a meditation or mindfulness workshop. The hour you spend there will serve you well in understanding who you are.

Being the real deal related to sales, and more specifically, cybersecurity sales are just as profound. Your clarity will be constantly refined through your authenticity, and your ability to use thought as a powerful tool will filter out the snakes within and around you. You will learn to shut down the voices that tell you that you suck. Your creativity will flourish, and you will find great solutions to the day-to-day challenges you face with ease. You will embrace it and have fun. What would cause you stress will now fill you with joy. You will be able to connect to various energies within any room and strategize how to approach and handle each energy, even if it conflicts with your own. You will shine, and shine bright because you live through you; that is your authentic self.

When a "real deal" cybersecurity sales professional engages with a client, they can build, develop and manage the relationship at a human level. They nurture and customize that relationship with a solid understanding of their product as such that they speak to it with experiential knowledge (even if they don't ever use it). The tools you use (in this case, product knowledge) give you the ability to speak naturally "off script," which amalgamates communication with your sales goal.

It's fascinating that all you are told as a child is just as relevant as an adult. In this case, the classic, 'be yourself' is everything!

CHAPTER EIGHT

DEVELOPING YOUR SALES PROCESS

Here's a way-back playback invitation to dive deep into the nook where your childhood memories are carefully stored.

Close your eyes (figuratively, not literally; you need your eyes open to read this excellent book). Go back to grade school and recall when you were tasked with an assignment that included presenting your work to your class.

Whatever the subject, whomever the teacher, and your presentation topic, the process was comfortably predictable.

You'd be given time to create an outline first. You'd then wiggle into the research phase. Once you had all the information you needed, you'd follow your teacher's flow, hop into the final draft, and prepare the presentation.

You practiced your presentation everywhere, including at the dinner table every day, in the washroom mirror to yourself, and at Aunty Hilda's potluck dinner. You had some sort of visual, a Bristol board with some neat pictures and white glue on it. You practiced your pitch until everything sounded just right!

On presentation day, you had everything ready to go, and if you were feeling fancy, you might have even planned to use the snazzy overhead projector that looked like E.T.'s cousin.

It was always a good time - until Little Johnny showed up to class with what could be his wedding suit on (yes, it was the obnoxious bow tie and freshly polished dress shoes).

Oh, Johnny, why did you wear the darn bow tie! It was bad enough that Johnny redefined the standard on Presentation Day.

The truth is, Little Johnny was a reminder of what you did not think of doing. He was the detail you forgot about, but through him, you picked up new strategies that you would implement in subsequent grades, making him awesome.

You still rocked your presentation because you worked hard and prepared. Also, you were a fine piece of unadulterated YOU, and Little Johnny could never replicate that. You always forgave Little Johnny for one-upping you in attire and shared your tooty-fruity recess snack with him because childhood is brotherhood.

Back to the now:

When was the last time you spoke in front of a group or at a public event?

How did you prepare?

Did you just show up and say whatever came to mind, or did you spend some time preparing to create a structured flow as you did back in grade school?

While I believe that there are talented masters of improvisation, I also firmly believe that preparation, especially a planned outline, is always helpful. A system and a sensible structure are essential to engage your listeners and inspire them to see the value of your presentation.

Like a good speech, the effort you put into your sales process needs to be structured. Efforts can always be seen and heard.

How can you build a sales process that aligns with your cybersecurity business objectives?

A sales process is a set of repetitive actions that you or your team takes from the point you acquire a lead to when you close the client, and it is pretty vital. It is the blueprint that determines conversion. A good sales process will provide you with a system that closes deals consistently.

The following seven stages in the cybersecurity sales process are designed to help you develop a sound, practical and strategic sales process.

So my friends, get ready to 'get ready' to sell like a superstar!

THE 7 STAGES IN THE CYBERSECURITY SALES MODEL

It is critical to learn the concept of "knowing your customer" as you can't use the same sales approach/technique with all your clients. For example, some clients are numbers people, and others might like to see the business value and technical details.

Mansour Khan

STAGE 1: PROSPECTING

WHAT YOU NEED TO KNOW:	WHAT YOU NEED TO DO:
Prospecting is an essential aspect of the sales process. A significant portion of your time will be invested in effective prospecting. This is the stage where you source for early-stage leads to work through the sales journey.	► Ensure you have scheduled time in your calendar to prospect. ► Research potential clients online or at industry events. ► Schedule an appointment with the prospective client. This can be virtual or in-person. ► Tap into your current network of clients and ask to be referred to people within their network who could benefit from cybersecurity products or services. ► Commit to innovation: remember to constantly innovate your marketing and search for prospects. ► Go all in! It is better to throw 100 rods in the lake to catch fish, versus just one.

STAGE 2: CONNECTING & QUALIFYING LEADS

WHAT YOU NEED TO KNOW:	WHAT YOU NEED TO DO:
During this stage, you will contact your leads to gather information about their business and requirements.	► Qualifying your early-stage leads is best done through a series of questions. These are the best questions to ask a B2B lead during the qualification phase.
With the information obtained, you will be able to qualify them and determine whether they are a good fit for your product or if you should guide them through the buyer's journey.	► What is your role in your organization?
In Human Resources (HR), recruitment is to hire the best candidate for the job; in sales, your objective is to acquire the best-fit lead.	► What challenges are you trying to overcome in your business? ► Why are these challenges a priority?
"If the lead does not fit, develop relationships and introduce your products and services for future opportunities." Mansour Khan	► Are there other solutions you are assessing?

STAGE 3: RESEARCHING A LEAD'S BUSINESS

WHAT YOU NEED TO KNOW:	WHAT YOU NEED TO DO:
The essence of research is to help you own your client's business to provide a customized solution and experience for them. This is where you learn more about your prospect and their business and it is an integral part of closing a deal. "Parallel to researching a client's business is researching them at a personal level. What are their interests, sports or other social likes and dislikes? Being able to relate personally is instrumental for developing a long-term relationship. Though it may not always be possible, a salesperson must always strive for it." Mansour Khan	▸ Do not be tempted to limit yourself to speaking ONLY with people in the security operation centre or the IT department. Doing so will prevent you from having a holistic understanding of your prospect's business. ▸ Engage with leaders of various departments to obtain a holistic view of the entire business operation. ▸ Do your research and ask all open-ended and closed-ended questions relevant to the objective. ▸ Determine what solution will best solve your client's needs accurately and to the best of your ability.

George Al-Koura has some great insight on Step 3: *opportunities to research and grow leads by investing in knowing your target client on a personal level are everywhere. As a sales professional, you should consider taking on social activities and hobbies that will allow you to interact with as many people as possible directly. For example, if trying to develop business locally and you discover through associates or research that the local Social Club has folks enrolled who work at professional, relevant organizations, it would serve your best business interests to consider joining that local house soccer or dodgeball league. People will always prefer to do business with those they know (and like)!*

Mansour Khan also has a valuable point, *it is critical to learn the concept of "knowing your customer/client" as you can't use the same sales approach/technique with all your clients. For example, some clients are numbers people, and others might like to see the business value and/or technical details.*

STAGE 4: DELIVERING BRILLIANT PITCHES

WHAT YOU NEED TO KNOW:	WHAT YOU NEED TO DO:
Now that you have a full working knowledge of your client's business, it is time to create your presentation and present a demo of your product or service.	▶ Ensure your client is 100% qualified as you don't want to waste your time or your client's time. ▶ Customize your presentation to address your client's pain points and requirements. ▶ Make it personal by pointing out specific issues they shared with you during the research stage. ▶ Consider using an onsite sales engineer to demonstrate what your client can expect when using your security product. This will also allow them to address any additional technical questions.

STAGE 5: HANDLING OBJECTIONS PROFESSIONALLY

WHAT YOU NEED TO KNOW:	WHAT YOU NEED TO DO:
You've presented, and now you engage in prospect-lead dialogue.	▸ Always go into a presentation meeting prepared to receive questions and concerns.
This part of the presentation will test your patience, knowledge, and persuasion. It is common to receive questions and queries at the end of your presentation. You should always expect more objections than agreeable feedback. Coming into the presentation prepared to handle potential objections is key. Your ability to be strategic with responses will enable you to customize your products to suit your client's needs.	▸ Understand that when people ask you questions, they are engaged. This is a great sign that indicates interest. This is the moment where you build a relationship of trust by offering honest answers that satisfy the customer's curiosity, intrigue, and concern.
	▸ Actively working with your team can help you plan and anticipate specific questions and objections. List all possible questions you may receive about cost, product features, functionality, and all other aspects of the proposed service. Prepare responses and review them often.
Though this stage can be one of pressure, choose to embrace it. All of the work you put in since the beginning culminates to this point.	▸ Always be ready to handle objections. Earning your client's satisfaction and trust during the exchange of objections and responses is the art of closing deals.
	▸ It will flow naturally when you master this process, and it becomes fun.
	▸ People may ask you redundant questions, provide a delay in responses, ask to change timelines or continuously request for more and more information. Manage and handle this process with patience and passion. Respect this process. Rebuttals to the objections need to be fully understood by you and mastered in delivery.

STAGE 6: CLOSING THE DEAL

WHAT YOU NEED TO KNOW:	WHAT YOU NEED TO DO:
This stage includes everything from sending a quote or proposal to negotiation or securing the buy-ins of the prominent decision-makers in your client's company. Be very careful with the pitfalls as the saying goes, "the devil is in the details," and this is one of those times you can get stung if you are not tactful. This is where a customer may share a different understanding of what you may or may not have said during the various stages of a sales journey. Remember, the deal is done, but the process is not over.	▸ Keep notes of every interaction you make with the customer (from the start of the sales journey to the end and beyond). ▸ Documenting and journaling detailed summaries of calls is the best way to ensure an accountable system is in place that manages the integrity of the relationship between yourself and your customer. This is what will help you remember everything you have said and promised. ▸ A successful sale involved compromise too so know that you may have wanted $$, and the client wanted X options — mutually beneficial means you both compromised to a level where each person has done the give and take to arrive there. ▸ Understand that though the deal is closed from your capacity, it still may have additional channels to go through, and until you are paid for the agreement, the deal should be considered a work in progress. It moves through other departments. Keep your eye on the deal as it travels through subsequent departments.

STAGE 7: NURTURING UPSELL & CROSS-SELL

WHAT YOU NEED TO KNOW:	WHAT YOU NEED TO DO:
While closing a sale is the main objective, that's not where leaders stop. That's where they begin. If you close a sale and you fail to nurture your clients, you have cut off the opportunities to up-sell and cross-sell your clients. Aside from that, I encourage that you build a formidable relationship with your clients and reinforce value to your clients. Most importantly, they become a client for life. They remember you, and guess what; they become your Rolodex. `	▶ Ensure you have built a healthy working relationship and friendly rapport with your clients. ▶ Reinforce value to your clients and provide them with the information they will value regarding their business and the additional services you can provide to enhance their experience. ▶ Be memorable. Whether it is through your personality or ability to relate and connect with your customer in a meaningful way, the impression and connection your client has with you and of you is what will sustain them as lifelong customers.

Karen Nemani sums up this final process, *"There's the sale then there's the steady state where customers need/want to feel heard. Successful salespeople take their customer comments back to their developers and turn customer challenges into organizational value propositions."* Such a valuable tip that has residual benefits.

Now that you understand how to develop a B2B sales process, the next step is a progression through optimization. The following section will highlight some of the best practices you can use to optimize your process for better results. The more you know, the more you grow!

DEVELOPING YOUR SALES PROCESS

STAGE 1: PROSPECTING

STAGE 2: CONNECTING & QUALIFYING LEADS

STAGE 3: RESEARCHING A LEAD'S BUSINESS

STAGE 4: DELIVERING BRILLIANT PITCHES

STAGE 5: HANDLING OBJECTIONS PROFESSIONALLY

STAGE 6: CLOSING THE DEAL

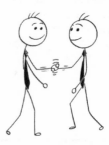

STAGE 7: NURTURING UPSELL & CROSS-SELL

BEST PRACTICES TO OPTIMIZE YOUR CYBERSECURITY SALES PROCESS

FIGURE OUT YOUR SALES PROCESS

*"Insanity is doing the same thing over and over
and expecting different results."*

Albert Einstein

If you want to close more deals, you need to align your sales process to fit the needs of your clients.

Conducting temperature checks periodically is a great way to ensure your sales process is effective. One of the many metrics you can use is demonstrated below:

Assess the last ten sales you have closed and ask yourself:

- What were they like from the onset to the end?

- What were the touchpoints with your clients?

- How long did the entire B2B sales process take? And,

- What was the timeframe between each stage?

Using measurable metrics to self-check is a fundamental skill that every successful cybersecurity salesperson demonstrates.

You can even use a simple timeline strategy as a metric for yourself. Once you have put the cybersecurity sales process into a timeline, check the timeframe for every sale you made. For instance, if you had ten clients who purchased your security products in five weeks, examine the average steps you need to take within that timeline.

Here's a template in reverse order,

- One week of deliberation before a signed contract ("*close the sale*") stage

- Three-to-five follow-up phone calls and emails (during the "*handling of objections*" stage)

- One demo (during the "*presentation*" stage)

- One phone call and two to three emails (during the "*researching*" stage)

- One discovery call (during the "*connecting and lead qualification*" stage)

- Two, welcoming warm emails and three phone calls to prospect (during the "*prospecting*" stage)

The above is only an example of a template. Create your process or speak to other sales leaders in your company and find out what they do, what works for them and what does not work for them. If they have a promising process, take those winning strategies and insert them within your process. Your senior peers and colleagues have been selling longer than you in that company. They understand the organization's ecosystem and the tools for marketing and tracking differently than you do. They have the blueprint figured out. Learn from it. Once you master the blueprint, you can always tweak and refine it to your liking. Remember never to stop innovating!

DESIGN CLIENTS' PERSONAS: BUYER'S JOURNEY

Mapping out a buyer's journey will enable you to view your sales process from your client's perspective, understand their pain points, and why your product or service is the best fit for them. Hashim Hussein provides a nice tip here:

Mapping the buyer's journey for your client's persona also affords you an insight into how to streamline your sales process to build good relationships with your clients and sell more. Using the MEDDIC framework is an excellent sales qualification methodology to help develop the right questions in the sales process. MEDDIC stands for Metrics, Economic Buyer, Decision Criteria, Decision Process, Identify Pain, Champion, and Competition. This is a key part of the sales process.

STATE THE ACTIONS THAT QUALIFY YOUR PROSPECT TO MOVE TO THE NEXT STAGE

You will need to define the metrics that get your prospects moved to the next stage in your sales process.

Remember, the prospect's actions and not your perception as a sales representative should lead the flow.

These questions can help evaluate the steps required:

- While warming your client, did you hit a particular pain point(s) that inspired your client to schedule a zoom meeting?

- While presenting the demo, were there questions that hindered the sales or features that enhanced progress?

- While pitching, did you get an instant 'yes' from the client? If so, figure out why it happened. Then, review how you developed the pitch and how you will use it again.

DESIGN THE EXIT METRICS FOR EVERY STEP IN THE CYBERSECURITY SALES PROCESS

What will be the exit metrics for every stage in the sales process? Figure out the events that need to occur to move your prospects from one stage to the next.

Let's say you are in the presentation stage. In this situation, you need a video testimonial of customers who have used your products before. You can share these videos with your prospects to move them to the 'closing' stage.

Here are some questions that you can ask yourself when defining the exit metrics required:

- Do I have complete information on how the product works?

- What actions should I take all through the stages of the sales process?

- What are the several ways conversations can be initiated?

- What should I say at every stage in the sales process?

- What are the different ways conversations could go, and how do I manage the flow?

- What type of content would my target prospects relate with?

These questions are crucial during the presentation stage where you need to engage your prospects with testimonials, videos, white papers, or case studies.

MEASURE THE OUTCOME OF THE SALES PROCESS

Your cybersecurity sales process needs to evolve as you move your prospects through the pipeline. As you progress with enhancing your sales process, you should assess your success.

You might want to know how prospects transitioned in and out of every stage during the process over time.

For example, suppose you had 75 prospects in January at the 'presentation' stage. You have moved 25 of them and added 15 more by the end of the month, leaving you with 65 prospects.

Consider the following metrics for various stages in your sales process:

- What's the average time prospects spent in each stage?

- What stage takes too long for them to transition.

- What's the percentage of prospects you close after presenting a demo?

- What percentage of prospects asked for a demo after the discovery call?

- What's the churn rate?

Most cybersecurity sales teams use these basic metrics in optimizing their sales process. You might need to think through specific metrics unique to the security product that can enable you to define success in a particular stage.

Another means of measuring your outcome is to use the three dimensions of success in the sales process. Figuring out your level in the following three dimensions' can offer you insights into what you need to know to revamp or optimize your sales process.

THE THREE DIMENSIONS

1. HUMMING

If you are closing 80% of sales or if 80% or more of sales reps in your team are meeting their monthly quota, then your sales process is humming. At this level, the entire team is performing well with no negative feedback concerning the sales process.

ASK YOURSELF: is your sales process humming? If you answered yes, congratulations, you have figured out the A to Z straight line process of executing a sale. My only advice is to keep improving because your competitors are around the corner, and if you don't keep innovating and marketing, we all know what happens.

2. EXPERIMENTING

At this level, your sales process is not humming. You are just testing what works and what does not.

For instance, you might be testing different channels in the 'connecting' stage to initiate discussions with your prospects. You can determine whether your client responds better to a Zoom meeting or a phone call. Figure it out quickly, and when you do, commit. If you need to make a tweak, make it. Always be improving!

3. THRASHING

When you use different presentation methods in the 'presenting' phase, it will be hard to know what works for most prospects. This is called 'thrashing', and it is not effective.

Remember, the sales process travels from point A to point Z in one solid line. Not a heartbeat. The line within the progress of the sales is linear.

You need to realize that a sales process is not a 'one shoe fits all' approach. There is no one perfect sales process. Every process needs to evolve to align with what you, your business, or prospects require.

You might already have a sales process you can enhance and improve with this great information! Follow along to learn how to create your cybersecurity sales process. Whether you are new to this world or a seasoned professional looking to grow, there is always something to learn!

CHAPTER NINE

BUILDING A CYBERSECURITY SALES PROCESS

"Predicting rain doesn't count. Building arks does."

Warren Buffett

What is the most powerful word?

Ask any parent what the most commonly used word is in their home. Most often, the answer will be the same throughout any age. That brilliant word is WHY.

Children are the most extraordinary learners because they are born with wonder. Their curiosity teaches them and carries them through every discovery and milestone.

Some of the most thoughtful questions arise from five-year-olds. Why doesn't the sun ever fall? Why do my feet have five toes? Why is water wet? Why is this the most powerful question? For every decision you make in each stage of your sales process, there's always a *why*. This is why building a sales process is essential. It lets you have a complete view of each step beforehand and know how it applies to your client's business. You can discover 'vulnerabilities' to understand what works, and match your sales process with your business expectations.

Using a fictional case study, I will walk you through how you can map your sales process.

BEGIN WITH THE END IN MIND

With every journey, therein lies a destination. With your cybersecurity sales process mapping, you must know where you are going and what you want to achieve. Your plan should be specific yet straightforward.

Example

Zulfiqar Networks is mapping its sales process; the Cybersecurity sales team has established their goal of increasing its win rate by 10% next quarter.

CREATE A BUY-IN AMONG ALL STAKEHOLDERS

Bring together other departments in your organization such as IT, customer service, marketing, and others and let them have a stake in your sales process. Don't limit the discussion of sales to your sales team. Let everyone share their goals and be involved throughout the process.

Example:

Zulfiqar holds a stakeholder meeting with the marketing team, sales team, product designers, customer experience leaders, and others. These teams contact potential, current, and future clients to determine the win rate.

OUTLINE THE STEPS IN YOUR SALES PROCESS

Using the sales process you developed, apply each step to your products. You can review the history of your current process.

- What steps generated the expected results?

- And where did prospects bounce?

- What is the average time spent in each step?

Working with your stakeholders, you can determine which team influences each step and the actions you and your team need to take to optimize the step.

Example:

Zulfiqar Networks' cybersecurity sales team mapped the six steps and has written down the actions to be taken in each stage. They have also assessed sales history in the past 12 months. This is where they can optimize their sales process to align with the new goal.

MAP THE BUYER'S JOURNEY

It's time to examine your sales process from your clients' perspective. Using the same template above, write down the actions and reactions you expect your clients to take or have. Pin your buyer personas somewhere or share them with everyone in the team so they can remain customer-centric.

Example:

By now, the sales team has mapped the client's journey in the context of their already defined sales process. This will enable the team to figure out areas of difficulties and inefficiencies, what steps are working, and what aspects need to be revamped.

Having mapped the cybersecurity sales process from your (seller) and the client's perspectives, you can now test it. Testing and evaluating the outcome will help you know the effectiveness of the process you have created.

Example:

Zulfiqar Networks' sales team tested its sales process. The team went through each stage and the relevant actions, and they preempted how clients reacted. As they transition through each step and move their objectives, they rejig the areas that are not working.

CYBERSECURITY SALES PROCESS VERSUS SALES METHODOLOGY

It is essential to differentiate cybersecurity sales processes and methodologies at this juncture. While they are closely related, a process is different from a methodology.

You should have a solid understanding of the sales process and its importance. Understanding methodology is a critical component of sales.

The methodology is a set of practices or a broader philosophy that inform how you build and conduct your sales process.

The following chapters will explain five major cybersecurity sales methodologies that you can leverage to develop and conduct your sales process.

CHAPTER TEN

DEMYSTIFYING THE CHALLENGER'S METHODOLOGY

"To drape instinct into garments of structure, embellished with purpose and fashioned with strategy, is to apply methodology."

Mahdi Raza

Buyers are empowered now, more than ever.

They have many ways to validate offerings and value propositions. Whether through leveraging search engines, or professional social networks, cybersecurity sales professionals need to account for all of this when engaging with any prospect.

Businesses thrive on relationships. Many people in the cybersecurity sales environment believe that building relationships with clients and prospects impacts the sales process significantly. There is a school of thought here on relationship selling versus methodology/process selling. Top salespeople have built relationships to help them create pipelines, but they always need to be a hunter in their DNA. Also, be hungry enough to close the deal. There are two types of sales reps: farmers and hunters. I would hire a hunter in a startup and a farmer for legacy technology where they would keep the customer happy.

According to them, if we were to contextualize this for the cybersecurity market, cybersecurity sales reps rarely use a relationship-building strategy; instead, they take control of the sales and teach the prospects what to do and how to overcome their challenges.

Research conducted by Gartner [6] revealed an emerging trend in the buyer's journey. The study discovered that clients had moved about 57% through the purchase process before contacting the sales rep. They have already researched and learned before entering the selling environment. They are already armed with their preconceived ideas, product features, and price; thus, they know what they want to pay.

The Challenger Model shines in this environment as clients are not interested in getting information about your products, features, and benefits. They are already confused with several options and choices, and they need to make a quick decision on which product to purchase. If they reach out to you or your sales team, they need answers to 'why'; they should subscribe to your solutions and not what to buy.

Should we then conclude that the Challenger Sales Methodology unlocks the latest buying trends?

Let's define the Challenger Selling system with a cybersecurity twist.

WHAT IS THE CHALLENGER SALES METHODOLOGY?

The Challenger sales methodology is built around a sales process where the sales team teaches, customizes, and takes charge of the entire sales experience. According to Adamson and Dixon [7], you need the right set of tools and training to take control of the conversation. You need to be a Challenger! So what does that mean?

Adamson, Dixon, and their team researched the behaviours and attitudes of several sales reps and profiled them into five distinct categories.

---

6 Gartner. 2019. "Challenger Sales Model Includes Training Reps in Three Behaviors." Gartner. https://www.gartner.com/smarterwithgartner/power-challenger-sales-model.

7 Shekhar, Arinjay. 2022 "The Challenger Sale Book Summary – A Quick 12 Min Readhttps://salesblink.io/blog/the-challenger-sale-book-summary

5 TYPES OF SALES PERSONALITIES

"The recognition of every flavour is the magic in every meal."

Mahdi Raza

It's essential to know your sales personality. Check out the five below and see where you fit.[8]

THE HARD WORKER: They 'Never say die;' they are self-motivated, they go above and beyond, they welcome feedback so long as it compliments their potential, and they prioritize self-improvement. They are committed to their craft, regardless of how hard it is. They are all in.

THE RELATIONSHIP BUILDER: They value connection and have a sincere interest in developing meaningful relationships. They go the extra mile to help people – especially clients. They are friendly, and they know how to build strong relationships. They enjoy working with everyone and understand how they can adjust their approaches to connect with anyone.

THE LONE WOLF: They work by instinct, are independent and do not rely on anyone. They are analytical and creative. They strategize silently and are highly focused. They make their moves based on intuition.

THE PROBLEM SOLVER: They are creative and topic-oriented. They pay attention to details and notice everything. They find challenges invigorating and are not afraid of failure. They are clever optimists and can provide multiple solutions to any problem.

THE CHALLENGER: They have a diverse perspective; they value opportunities that allow them to understand the client's business. They are confident and can ask difficult questions and debate. They are charismatic and subtle leaders. They have a knack for inspiring the client to make leaps.

....

8   Mares, Justin. 2021. "A 5-Minute Summary Of "The Challenger Sale" Book Your Boss Told You To Read." HubSpot Blog. https://blog.hubspot.com/sales/challenger-sale-summary.

A Challenger profile allows the cybersecurity sales team to create constructive tension and disrupt their client's thinking in a bid to force them to take on or 'adopt' a new perspective. As challengers inspire their clients to consider new ideas, they can present them with an alternative.

To be a Challenger, you need to offer insights about new ideas, emerging trends, and inspiring opportunities within your client's industry. Above all, you need to be aligned with all of this by having valuable solutions that can be implemented.

You need to capture their beliefs and assumptions, dissect the flaws, and create better solutions. This disruptive thinking will boost your sales and help you meet your quotas.

HOW CAN YOU LEVERAGE THE CHALLENGER SELLING TECHNIQUE

As technologies evolve and security products and solutions become more complex, so does the sales process. Clients can now ask Siri or Alexa to supply detailed information about a product, service, industry, or company. This means they are researching before reaching out to salespeople. This is a complex sales situation, and the Challenger approach is the best way to handle it.

A study[9] with over 6,000 sales reps surveyed unveiled these interesting findings:

- 40% of top-of-the-board salespeople are using Challenger selling.

- Top Sales Reps are two times more likely to employ a Challenger approach than any other method.

- 50% of top performers are challengers when it comes to complex sales.

- 75 % of top performers adopt a Relationship Building style.

Therefore, we can conclude based on these statistics that the client's buying experience determines the success of any sales methodology you

---

9   Mares, Justin. 2021. "A 5-Minute Summary Of "The Challenger Sale" Book Your Boss Told You To Read." HubSpot Blog. https://blog.hubspot.com/sales/challenger-sale-summary.

choose. You will achieve poor results if you leverage a relationship-based method to deal with complex sales situations.

Using Challenger's approach will allow you and your sales team to close the most complex sales in your funnel.

Aside from the positives, are there downsides to the Challenger Sales Methodology?

While Cybersecurity Salespeople who adopt this approach drive sales via constructive tension, the approach is ineffective for the average performing or intermediate rep; or when a product or solution possesses a simple sales cycle.

It is essential to review your prospect's requirements and background to determine if challenger selling is suitable.

HOW TO USE 'REFRAME' TO BECOME A CHALLENGER

It does not matter which category you or any sales team member falls into. You can teach yourself and your team how to adopt the challenger approach. One way of achieving this is using what I call 'Reframe'. Reframing enables each team member to think like a teacher and not a relationship builder.

How do you achieve this as a sales leader?

Begin with any item you can lay your hands on in your war room. It could be pens, flash drives, staplers, books, light bulbs, or notepads. Put them into a bag and ask each team member to pick an item. This item will be the product they will be selling to their fictional clients. You can use worksheets to track ideas all through the exercise.

For a team member who picks a flash drive, a common approach to selling would be product-centric. The person would generally position the item as "a perfect way to prevent data loss or access data anywhere." However, you can teach your team to use the Challenger selling via a scenario that looks like this:

TEACHING POINT

"Several people save important files and data on their laptop or computers. However, do you know if malware infiltrates the system, they can lose those files with little or no chance of data recovery?"

If the prospects typically save their work on a computer without backing it up elsewhere, they will be piqued by the teaching point.

THE WARMER POINT

"Our clients often tell us they constantly lose important information on their laptop devices. They tell us they need to consider other options to save their files so they can easily access them on other devices. Are you facing a similar issue?"

This will enable you to validate your prospects and compel them to share their issues about backup and data loss prevention issues.

I am using a flash drive as an imaginary item, not necessarily saying it is the best backup solution.

REFRAME

Many clients take measures to save their data on every device. Some send files to Google drive or email, while others install malware protection, which is excellent. It is still important to note that in the case of theft or system failure, you would still have a backup of essential files and data, which you can access from any device before connecting to the internet. Do you know you can even plug your flash drive into your mobile device and download your files from the flash drive?

What's the important file you wouldn't want to lose?

If you notice, the last question is there to connect your prospect emotionally.

EMOTIONAL CONNECTION

"That's exciting! One of my friends also can't afford to lose his eBook collections. Sadly, his flash drive is full, and he might need another one. Is that the case for you?"

Once your prospect discovers that you demonstrate empathy about securing what's important to them, you have the perfect opportunity to introduce your product.

VALUE PROPOSITION: "Well, you will be excited to know you can save as many books and interesting movies as possible without the fear of data loss. For instance, you used to save 1000 books on your 2GB flash drive. By acquiring a 16 GB flash drive, you can save more books and collect more movies. Is this something you would like to try?"

Then all you have to do at this point is to share your product.

VALUE PROPOSITION: "That's interesting! We are presently running a promo where you can buy two flash drives for one. I would be glad to talk to you about how you can save more files and organize your data with this exciting opportunity. Is that something you would want me to share more info on?"

After taking the sales team through these exercises, get everyone to share feedback.

- *Did each member guide the prospect to the solution effectively?*

- *How did they uniquely reframe the problem to the conventional way of selling?*

Using the available items with your sales team has proven how the Challenger selling method can be used in a complex selling environment. It's time to dive deeper so you can use the method to sell any of your products or services.

NOTE: I am a huge fan of an assumptive call to action value proposition closer. Read that again. Here is an example, "That's interesting! We are presently running a promo where you can buy two flash drives for one. I would be glad to talk to you about how you can save more files and organize your data with this exciting opportunity. Should I email you the brochure, pricing and how to have it shipped within 24 hours on your abc@abc.com email address?"

5 EASY-TO-FOLLOW STEPS TO LEVERAGE THE CHALLENGER SALES METHODOLOGY

Don't forget, the Challenger Selling approach is about teaching prospects rather than building relationships.

You need to arm yourself to take charge of the sale and nudge prospects to make a buying decision. This method dives into the prospect's fears and unlocks what happens when they fail to act. It also inspires them to see your product as the solution to their present predicaments.

Here are five steps to adopt the Challenger Selling methodology:

STEP #1 THE WARM-UP

This is where you build credibility with your prospects. You need to demonstrate that you understand their challenges and emphasize them. You can do this by researching their pain points, requirements, and the issues they are facing. For instance, if they have just suffered from their third ransomware attack in the space of six months, your product should prioritize this main challenge over others.

QUICK TIPS:

- Let them know why you are reaching out: Discuss typical issues they are currently facing to show you understand their pain points.

- Position yourself as an expert: Demonstrate that you possess the experience to understand and empathize.

- Get them to feel curious: Use facts and statistics related to issues that interest them.

- Go Interactive: Deploy visuals and highly interactive content to involve them in the discussion so you can uncover their pain points. It could be a gamified survey or short questionnaires where they can earn rewards for selecting appropriate answers. They can use the rewards to claim a promo on any of your products.

- Every conversation with your prospects should be thought-provoking. The investment in this conversation will serve as the foundation for leading your prospects further in the buyer's journey.

STEP #2 REFRAME THE CONVERSATION

The prospect might have mentioned their most significant challenge during warm-up: securing their endpoints or preventing data loss. This phase deals with digging deeper into the root of their challenges and reframing them as an opportunity to grow.

Try to dissect any flaw or misconception they may have related to how they intend to solve their problems. As you introduce a new view into the discussion, your prospect will begin to have a mind shift and embrace new ways to solve their problems.

Before the conversation ends, you are already telling your prospect that the solution they have researched or conceived is not practical. After challenging your prospect to accept your idea, you can start reframing the conversations around better options.

QUICK TIPS:

- Deal with the issue of concern raised by your prospects in Step One and reiterate knowledge, experience, and understanding.

- Challenge your prospects to take on a new perspective that is more effective on how to solve their problem.

- Deal with the issues with confidence. The more relatable and confident you are, the more your prospects will trust you to embrace your alternative ideas or solutions.

- Take note that your aim at this stage is not to sell but to create/encourage a high sense of curiosity in your prospects until they start changing their perspectives.

STEP #3 LEVERAGE EMOTIONS

Regardless of how effective your product or service is, emotions will still define the B2B purchasing behaviour regardless of how effective your product or service is. According to Prof. Gerald Zaltman[10], 95% of our decision-making is driven by our emotions and subconsciousness. The more prospects can PERSONALLY connect with your solution, the more likely they will be to buy it.

One means of getting your prospects to connect with your products and see how they will benefit from them is to share relatable customer stories. You can share a story of a company that used your endpoint security product with similar problems. This will make your prospect perceive themselves as the character. By revealing how the product helped your previous client, you challenge them to see how it will benefit them as well.

Once they realize a better solution will take care of their pain points, they will find it difficult to return to their previous thought pattern.

Now that your prospects can see themselves utilizing the new solution, you can guide them on an emotional trip of what will happen if they stick with the new way of thinking.

QUICK TIPS:

- Tell a story: Storytelling evokes some emotional effect. Share a story of what prospects should expect if they follow their conventional path. Ensure the story is relatable and hits the pain points prospects are facing.

- Use client stories: Use real-life stories of the successful application of your product to replace the fictional sad ending. Back the stories up with case studies of individuals who have attempted to solve their problems with alternative means. You can use visuals to make the pictures stick in their minds instead of words when pitching or presenting.

- Research: At this point, supply relevant insights that resonate with the aspirations and concerns of your prospects. They

10 Chierotti, Logan. 2018. "Harvard Professor Says 95% of Purchasing Decisions Are Subconscious." Inc. Magazine. https://www.inc.com/logan-chierotti/harvard-professor-says-95-of-purchasing-decisions-are-subconscious.html.

immediately start picturing themselves using your product. Back up your presentation with relevant data to new ways to rationalize your statements.

- This is where all your efforts begin to produce results. Your prospects will find it hard backsliding or sticking to conventional solutions if you do it right.

STEP #4 THE VALUE PROPOSITION

This is the time to show your prospects the better future they would have if they followed the new path you are presenting. Don't introduce your product yet, but focus on delivering to your prospect how their challenges will be solved.

You are on the journey with them because you are selling them something. You have to be genuine at this stage as value is also felt by human emotion. Keep in mind; that people buy from people whom they like. Delivering value with a real human connection and genuine care to solve their problem is felt by your customer and builds trust and appreciation. Their success is your success, and your success is theirs. They know you get paid for their problem being solved. If you come across as a snake oil salesperson, or if there are alternative products, you can kiss the deal goodbye.

QUICK TIPS:

- Paint a positive picture of the future: Flip the story you shared in the last step about the unhappy ending to show the prospect what they will experience if they decide to act now.

- Focus on the solution: Don't present the product. Let your prospects connect the dots independently.

- Clarify any ambiguity: Take out time to answer every question. You can guide your prospects in connecting the dots.

- Your main objective is to educate your prospects on what their problem looks like – ideally without presenting your product. If you manage this stage well, your prospect will buy into the solution before presenting your product.

5 EASY-TO-FOLLOW STEPS TO LEVERAGE THE CHALLENGER SALES METHODOLOGY

STEP #1 THE WARM-UP

STEP #2 REFRAME THE CONVERSATION

STEP #3 LEVERAGE EMOTIONS

STEP #4 THE VALUE PROPOSITION

STEP #5 THE PRODUCT

STEP #5 THE PRODUCT

You put in the effort, understood the prospect's challenges, reframed them, gained their trust, and presented a solution to address the challenges. What you need to do now is to let them know you have the exact solution.

If you follow steps 1-4, step 5 should be easy and quick. What you sell determines how you will present the product. If you are selling a SaaS product, you can provide the prospect with a demo. If you are a content development agency in the cybersecurity space, you can show them similar client projects you have worked on and feedback from the clients.

HOW TO APPLY CHALLENGER SELLING

Now, I will show you how to apply Challenger selling in a fictional setting.

You are talking to the CEO of Zareen Inc., whose company has experienced several downtimes due to malware attacks; you may discover the root cause to be an insider threat. While digging further, you realize the prospect already believes installing new malware protection is the only way to secure critical infrastructure.

Armed with this information, you can position yourself as an expert in cybersecurity training and awareness. You can also use data to showcase the reasons for the problem's existence. You can then reframe the issue by explaining to the prospect that installing malware protection works in a, b, and c scenarios. Still, their business does not fall into any of the categories.

The prospect will be shocked by this discovery. You can now present the best methods and alternatives to solving the problems. This action will help the prospects shift their paradigms on securing their endpoints against insider threats and external threats.

At this point, you can share compelling stories to draw/attract the attention of your prospects as they begin using the alternatives and connecting to the stories you are sharing. You can inject emotions by showing them what will happen if they do not embrace the new direction.

Then bring out case studies backed up by real data to buttress how other people in the same situations have chosen the new direction or solution to solve their security challenges. Your prospects will start seeing the solutions as the most reasonable step to take, and they will be eager to know how to start.

Finally, present your product, cybersecurity and awareness training for all employees, and provide valuable insights on how they can save money when everyone in the organization is educated about best practices and strategies in cybersecurity.

The bottom line is that before you present your product, you would have positioned it as the only choice, and the prospects would make the buying decision on the spot.

If you enjoyed this chapter, then please join me in the next chapter as I unveil another methodology known as 'solution selling'.

CHAPTER ELEVEN

CYBERSECURITY SOLUTION SELLING TO NON-SECURITY CLIENTS

CFO, CIO OR OTHER BUSINESS UNIT LEADERS

"There is a significant communication gap when the customer internal security team is asked to pitch why the business needs this solution. As a vendor, the security director has a challenge in communicating why they are buying a solution that helps the business financially, and also impacts their security, operation and the overall impact on their customer"

Hashim Hussein

As a cybersecurity salesperson, you are conversant with 'Solution Selling.' Perhaps that's the strategy you are presently using. This sales methodology was popularized in the 1980s. Like a doctor, the salesperson diagnoses a patient's issue and prescribes the correct solution to cure the problem.

The patient (client) may not know they have the sickness, nor understand the level of severity or how urgent it is and how to cure it. As a salesperson, you are discussing with a prospect who has experienced data breaches such as five attacks in the span of one year. The prospect may not be aware of the consequences of not complying with General Data Protection Regulation (GDPR) and other standards. You are an essential resource that can assist the prospect to understand and take the necessary action, or the prospect risks penalties for violation. Remember, cybersecurity is a new and complicated space where the threat is rapidly evolving, and the landscape is constantly changing. In layman's terms, you need to be able to provide the most concise and digestible information and solution. People buy from people who make sense to them.

Kush has a great tip, salespople should build a business case deck in plain English ready to give to the client (CISO, CIO, etc.) to better enable them to communicate the value. A one-page executive slide should also be developed for non-technical executives.

WHAT IS CYBERSECURITY SOLUTION SELLING?

Cybersecurity solution selling is a sales approach where cybersecurity salespeople assess a prospect's needs to recommend specific products or solutions that can solve their problems and take care of their concerns. Mansour Khan has some advice on solution selling:

As a cybersecurity salesperson, you have a complete overview of your prospect's situations and have thought about them. You don't want to sell just to meet your monthly quota, but you want to go deeper. This is where knowledge comes in. You need to understand your prospects' industry, the unique issues that similar clients have faced, and their overall objectives for having the problems resolved. In addition to all this, the salesperson or the company he is representing has to be an expert in Cyber Security and not just their product in situations where they want to provide an end-to-end strategy.

When is the best situation to use solution selling?

Mansour proposes the following, "Solution selling works best for a business with highly branded packages or products, aiming to align with complex target customers' needs. If your company provides a cloud-based service coupled with security and maintenance, you can have different packages for your clients."

As a cybersecurity salesperson, you need to know the amount of data your client needs to store, the number of devices accessing these files, and what other features, functionality, and support the client will require.

A well-executed solution selling strategy focuses on the bigger picture. The aim is not to sell product features and specs but solutions. The 'why' is prioritized over the 'what'.

What you are offering is not as significant as why the client needs it.

Here's a hypothetical example:

Hyder Consulting is a cybersecurity consulting firm that provides cybersecurity risk assessment for midsize and large-scale retail enterprises.

Here's a conventional way the sales team will sell in the evaluation- emphasize the various benefits of the solution the firm offers:

"Our risk assessment covers every form of risk businesses face and enables them to figure out where they need to make improvements. In a nutshell, we help businesses to be more secure."

This is selling the product.

Suppose the Hyder Consulting Sales team wants to sell the solution and not the product. It will highlight or bring forth the various every day risks in the prospect's industry, highlight different cyber threats a business like that of the client faces and talk about the aspects of risk assessments that deal with those areas. It would provide a vivid picture of how the company can progress by engaging with Hyder Consulting.

That approach might take the following form:

"We realize that retail organizations like yours employ workers who aren't security experts and could be prone to phishing and other social engineering attacks. We simulate those breaches using penetration testing in our assessment. This is to detect unknown vulnerabilities in your systems and operations- coupled with other solutions that deal with other risk eventualities."

"With remarkable track records of collaborating with clients in your industry and actionable solutions that we provide with our assessment, we can help you secure your critical infrastructure, train your employees, and take out vulnerabilities that can jeopardize the security and safety of your business transactions and retail operations."

These two approaches explain the difference between *what* and *why*. It describes your service and projects and why it is valuable to your prospect.

HOW TO APPLY SOLUTION SELLING

Here is your prospects' business factor plan you can use to get started with solution selling.

1. FIGURE OUT THE CLIENT'S PAIN POINTS

Identifying your client's pain points is a significant aspect of the process. You need this information to target your prospects and present your solution effectively.

You can review the past sales you have closed to uncover the issues prospects faced that prompted them to buy your product or subscribe to your service.

2. CREATE YOUR QUESTIONS

Once you have identified the pain points addressed by your products or service address, the next step is to create questions to help diagnose them.

- *What prompted your decision to collaborate with us?*

- *When did you finalize resolving the issue?*

The cybersecurity sales professional should think about the positive business outcome for the client.

- *What are the desired outcomes of a potential solution to your current issues?*

- *What do you want to get out of my product?*

CLIENT: *"We want it to detect and automate threat hunting - to give time back to our security analysts. We also want to minimize the dwell time of attacks."*

The cybersecurity sales professional now has two critical outcomes to think about:

1. *Make analysts more productive, and give them time back.*

2. *Catch threats as early as possible.*

Two outcomes:

- *Reduce administration time, and increase productivity of the team. TIME + MONEY= Savings*

- *Minimize company Risk*

A strategic approach is preparing the right questions beforehand; this will focus the conversation on the client instead of your offerings.

Begin with broad and open-ended questions, as they will enable you to investigate important aspects of your prospects' business. Then narrow it down to find specific facts and figures to build a strong case for your product.

3. SELL VALUE AND SOLVE THE BUSINESS PROBLEM.

Solution selling is effective because it does not focus on product features or price tags but on ROI. The R always has to be bigger than I. The bigger it is, the easier the Value is to present.

You need to understand and demonstrate the value of your products. Here are some questions that can help you achieve this:

- *Is your product making life easier? What tasks or problems are being taken care of?*

- *Does your product save clients time? How much time is saved?*

- *What could users achieve within those timeframes?*

- *Do clients save money by using your product? How much could be achieved with this amount?*

- *How does your product or service influence how users perceive your client's brand? Do they look more efficient, credible, proactive, or successful?*

- *How does your product impact the client's bottom line six months or years after buying?*

You can highlight the answers to all these questions when discussing them with your prospects.

Let's examine the *Sales Process Lifecycle*.

SOLUTION SELLING SALES PROCESS

While the process used today can be broad, we provide a streamlined process that top sales performers who use solution selling employ.

PROSPECT: Find clients that have problems your product can solve.

QUALIFY: Know the stakeholders responsible for making decisions called the demand-unit, buying centre, or decision-making unit.

DISCOVER: Diagnose your client's requirements.

ADD VALUE: Create a client champion; connect the buying centre.

SHARE: Present a custom solution and showcase the return on investment.

CLOSE: Reach a mutual agreement that benefits both parties.

You can call this a cheat sheet, but it works for solution selling.

Below are some solutions selling questions to accurately investigate and diagnose your clients' pain points.

Figure out the root causes: What factors are causing pain for your prospects?

ESTIMATE THE EXTENT: How is this pain impacting your prospect, their business, employees, and the entire company? How many individuals will enjoy the ease of living when the problems are solved?

SECURE BUY-IN: Assess the buyer's interest in your product or service. Are they excited that your product can alleviate their pain?

These sample questions will provide insight into each objective:

FIGURE OUT THE ROOT CAUSES:

- *How has the (pain) degenerated to the (present state)?*

- *How important is the (issue)?*

- *Have you realized the (yet-to-be-considered factors) affecting the (pain or problem)?*

ESTIMATE THE EXTENT:

- *How has this pain influenced your (daily or weekly) productivity?*
- *What is the opinion of (job title) about this pain or issue?*

SECURE BUY-IN:

- *In an ideal world with no (issue, pain, or problem) of such, what's unique about your outcomes, priorities, and overall success of your business?*
- *We can solve (pain) with a Y solution.*
- *What's your take on this?*

CHAPTER TWELVE

MAHDI'S CYBERSECURITY SELLING SYSTEM

"Life is an accumulation of moments. The interpretation of those moments nurtures our individual uniqueness."

Mahdi Raza

When you have a chance, visit your local art gallery with a few friends. Stop at each display and silently contemplate the essence of the piece. Then, exchange thoughts with one another. You'll be amazed at how different your views are. Even though you are looking at the same thing, you are not looking at the same thing! You get to learn a lot about yourself and the world through simple adventures. It keeps your perspective challenged, and through the challenges, you evolve.

Sales are the same. Everyone will have a perspective. Each perspective offers value. Through my unique journey relating to sales, I have immersed myself into hundreds and hundreds of pages that provided insights into selling. I have watched tons of videos and movies for entertainment and informational purposes. I have met unique and inspirational sales leaders, coaches, mentors, and trainers.

More than that, I am my extraordinary accumulation of moments and experiences. I am a parent as well. I have collaborated with other parents and studied the art of how to sell a desired behavioural outcome to a child successfully. On the flip side, I have been amazed at the creativity children (including mine) pitch at their parents when they need parental buy-in.

I enjoy being observant and contemplative. Have you noticed how people space and zone out at a gas station while pumping gas? I have often wondered what they think about while waiting for the fuel to hit the top. Do they think about the laundry? Or the football game? What to have for dinner? What did their boss say to them earlier that day? Maybe they are like me and are wondering what I am wondering as I wonder about them.

Human behaviour and the ability to silently observe is a thrill.

During my snazzy pre-car era, I enjoyed commuting via public transportation. Growing up in Scarborough, I would often take the TTC bus to the Kennedy (central) Subway Station and end up at Eaton Centre in downtown Toronto. I would give myself some extra time to dazzle my boyish beauty (because you never know whom you will meet) at home before leaving and stopping at the food court to grab a snack or meal. I'd find a bench somewhere to enjoy a few quiet minutes to myself before getting to work. While I sat there, I would unintentionally find myself 'people watching.' That is a simple observation of conduct and behaviours. I am fortunate to have grown up in a multicultural part of Ontario, and the diversity I was exposed to was phenomenal and fantastic. Go to a mall one day and sit on the bench with a fancy food court snack. People watch. See what you learn about yourself through others. The world is the greatest teacher.

Back to sales. I have had the pleasure of learning through observation and understanding the processes that work for successful sales leaders (and don't work). I have paid close attention to their individualistic flare by means of adding their unique twists. Everyone has their twist on everything important to them. Think about the secret sauce used in many fast-food chains, especially deep-fried chicken. The secret is that it is always a little different than the rest. Not necessarily better or worse, but unique indeed.

To get into my unique selling system, you must first accept and understand that top sales performers know how to handle objections from their clients. Knowing this is a prerequisite to the information you are about to absorb. You need to understand your product, but more importantly, know those objections better.

"Good sales reps are seen as trusted advisors in the eyes of their clients. And really good ones carry those relationships for their whole career. Whether they work at vendor X now or Y later - clients they've built strong relationships with will follow." — David Mahdi

Invest in developing and asking the right questions while qualifying your lead against trying to force a product on a prospect, especially when they don't need it.

I love this approach because of its uniqueness and emphasis on mutual trust between you and the clients. It means your clients can trust you, and you wouldn't recommend a product that does not align with their requirements. Your clients also see you as advisors who assess their challenges using questioning methods during the qualification stage.

Once you realize your product won't address the clients' pain points, the system says you should not convince them.

Just abort!

If you look at this selling system, the client ends up convincing you to sell and not the other way around. Two types of sales happen. Either you sell them something, or they sell you on why they don't want what you are selling.

My Selling System has three primary stages: relationship building, qualification and closing. I have tweaked and modified the process over the years, and I am going to break it down into seven simple steps.

1. RAPPORT BUILDING

This is the first stage in relationship building, where you build a rapport with your prospect. Communication should be open and honest. People buy from people whom they like. Energy attracts energy. Regardless of the format of the meeting — whether in person or over video — be on time, be ready, smile, be positive, smell good, dress well, and play the part.

Example:

MAHDI: *Hello, Fatimah. This is Mahdi from siberX. I hope all is well and you are enjoying the fantastic weather; thank you for setting up this time to chat. Is this a convenient time to talk?*

FATIMAH: *Hey, Mahdi. Yes, it is lovely outside; I had been anticipating your call.*

MAHDI: *Awesome! Let's start with understanding what your business does. I have done my research. I would love to hear from you.*

FATIMAH: *Of course! We are an IT education company. We provide digital transformation and cybersecurity training for mid-level enterprises.*

2. SET UP

The next stage is to set roles and expectations, ground rules, and a comfortable atmosphere where business dealings occur.

Example:

MAHDI: *I learned a lot about what you do from our last conversation, Fatimah. I would love to know more about your training modalities. How do you research prospects, and what platforms do you use to train their employees or organize training and awareness events for your target audience?*

FATIMAH: *Sure, Mahdi.*

Setting expectations is essential; however, keep in mind, that this is where you are genuinely getting to know about their problems, challenges and thoughts.

3. PAIN

This third step transitions you to the qualification phase. Having built rapport and established clear expectations, it is time to investigate the pain points and concerns your prospects face.

This aspect of the communication will enable you to figure out why your product or service is the best fit for the prospect.

MAHDI: *Fatimah, I feel the main reason some of your leads don't subscribe to training is that there are a lot of online courses that address different cybersecurity topics. However, none of them are customized to address your unique challenges. Because of that, you have been recording cases of insider threats due to negligence on the part of your employees.*

FATIMAH: *That sounds right. Recently, we missed three major deals because of the downtime caused by a data breach, and we presently have a fine to pay for violating GDPR. We did not know anything about GDPR until we were summoned.*

4. BUDGET

This stage typically comes last in most systems. However, in my selling system, it is where you discuss the budget and commitment.

You should find out if your clients can afford your product or service. If they can't, the best thing is to save your time and avoid selling to them.

It is not only the budget you consider; you also need to investigate if they are willing and ready to invest time and commit resources to solve their issues/challenges. The best way to find out is to just ask them.

MAHDI: *Fatimah, we have figured out the root cause of your challenges. I have explained how our VR Education for Cybersecurity can help you train your employees in an immersive environment. May I know your budget for training your team of 50 leaders in an interactive and immersive environment without leaving your company premises/in a work-from-home environment?*

FATIMAH: *We currently spend $20 per month to train each employee on identified topics in Cybersecurity that improve their skills and knowledge on how to manage security incidents and phishing attacks. We can afford between $15 and $20.*

MAHDI: *Well, I am glad to inform you that you will save money as our enterprise plan is perfect for you, and it will cost you $19 to train a team of 50.*

5. DECISION

This is the last phase in the qualification stage where you discuss *who, what, why, where* and *how* your prospects want the buying process to flow.

Example:

MAHDI: *I believe the Enterprise plan will ensure all your employees have access to cybersecurity training with group discussions, real-life scenarios management and customized modules that address specific issues you are facing presently.*

FATIMAH: *Yes, I think the Enterprise plan is ideal for us.*

MAHDI: *That's great! I will set you up; in the meantime, I recommend you check our website siberx.org to register for free training and events your team can familiarize themselves with. I believe this will enable you to have a first-hand experience of what to expect in our customized training.*

6. FULFILLMENT

This is where you present your product or service as the best solution to address your client's needs. Your proposal will meet their requests, especially in line with their budget and the decision-making procedures.

Ensure that your proposal reflects what you have learned about their pain points during the qualification stage.

MAHDI: *Hey Fatimah, have you enrolled your team for our events on siberx.org?*

FATIMAH: *Yes. I saw the security awareness training in a gamified method, and it was terrific. We are ready to enroll in customized VR training.*

7. POST-SELL

It's time to close the deal. Establish the next points of action and prevent losing the deal to competition. You can also upsell your client on another solution.

MAHDI: *Thank you, Fatimah, for choosing siberX VR Cybersecurity Education for Enterprise. I am positive our innovative and immersive training is the best for your company. If you need any assistance, feel free to reach out; you have my number.*

FATIMAH: *Definitely, Mahdi. I appreciate your help.*

MAHDI: *It's a pleasure. In our discussion, we also discussed pen-testing. I want you to know that we can test your system and network to detect vulner-*

MAHDI'S CYBERSECURITY SELLING SYSTEM

1. RAPPORT BUILDING

2. SET UP

3. PAIN

4. BUDGET

5. DECISION

6. FULFILLMENT

7. POST-SELL

abilities and help you develop mitigation strategies. I think that would also help secure your critical infrastructures against cyber-attacks.

FATIMAH: *Sure, Mahdi. I will consider that and get back to you.*

As a Cybersecurity Salesperson, you aim to move from one stage to the next to reach the final stage efficiently and effectively.

While the Mahdi Selling System also covers methodologies that emphasize building relationships with your clients above, I wanted to highlight the method for understanding your clients and their business. The system enables you to qualify your leads and prevent selling to the wrong set of people.

CHAPTER THIRTEEN

CONSULTATIVE SELLING: METHODOLOGY SELLING BASED ON CLIENTS' NEEDS

Sales automation is presently optimizing inside selling strategies, and a lot of top performers in the sales industry are leveraging this new trend to achieve better results with their sales process. A 2018 survey [11] conducted by KCBM Technology Group described this fact - companies who depend primarily on inside sales tend to endeavour to outgrow their competitors who rely on field sales.

WHAT DOES IT MEAN TO SELL BASED ON A CLIENT'S NEED?

In the traditional approach, salespeople highlight how their products and services can address a client's pain points without understanding the pain. A need-based approach magnifies the specific interests of clients in the sales process. The sales process is all about the client. In contrast, consultative selling is a form of need-based selling that prioritizes

11 KeyBanc Capital Markets. 2019. "2019 KBCM SaaS Survey." KeyBank. https://www.key.com/kco/images/2019_KBCM_saas_survey_102319.pdf.

relationship and rapport building with clients with the main intention of understanding their interests and requirements rather than selling. By focusing on building a personal connection with clients, you are setting yourself up for well-rounded interactions and future collaboration with your prospects.

WHAT IS CONSULTATIVE SELLING?

Consultative selling is a methodology that prioritizes the building of trust and creation of value with a prospect and exploring their pains before recommending a solution. As a cybersecurity salesperson, your first goal is to build a cordial relationship, and the next goal is to recommend the right product.

This selling approach works for an insider sales strategy where you need to uncover your client's needs in real-time and present compelling solutions.

HOW TO APPLY CONSULTATIVE SELLING STRATEGY

There are seven ways to successfully apply the consultative selling strategy.

1. INJECT INSIGHTS INTO QUESTIONS

The first step is to understand your client's requirements with open-ended questions. You need to create a detailed picture of what they need to enable both parties to agree on best-fit solutions.

While you need to ask your client questions, that process may take time, and it may look like an interrogation that can bore clients stiff. You can introduce relief by offering insights as you ask questions.

For example, if you are selling an endpoint security product to a prospect, your conversation may digress to training and development.

In that case, asking questions about malware protection wouldn't cut it. Rather, you can briefly discuss how you have trained clients on best practices when using malware protection before proceeding.

This puts you in the position to ask the questions. Injecting insights rather than following a structured template offers a rationale and helps you build credibility.

2. DEVELOP KNOWLEDGE-BASED TRUST

COVID-19 has changed the way people communicate globally; we are seeing more remote engagements between sellers and their clients. While it might look impossible to build trust without in-person interaction, you can surmount this challenge by building a knowledge-based trust.

WHAT IS A KNOWLEDGE-BASED TRUST?

This is a trust emanating from actions that align with words.

Try to follow up at least after the first call. You can reach out to your prospects, letting them know it was a pleasure speaking to them; reiterate some specific concerns that came up in the last discussion and remind them to call or send you a chat in case they have questions.

The essence of the follow-up is to show your clients that you are reliable, emphatic and that you keep your words.

That way, you can build an open, solid and cordial relationship with your client and your product censors as valuable.

3. KEEP YOUR COMMUNICATION CONVERSATIONAL REAL

The trust-building process goes beyond familiarizing yourself with the client's business. You would need to appear approachable, emphatic and be disarming. It has to be obvious that you care about what you sell and whoever wants to buy it. It means speaking excitedly and from the heart.

Keep your prospect engaged all through the conversation, and don't try to put on a fake smile just to push a product down the neck of your prospect. You need to be real and believe in yourself and your product to the extent that you can discuss it with all honesty and genuine conviction.

If you are selling an antivirus, don't try to convince your client it can protect them against a ransomware attack. Only speak to your product value and endeavour to connect with your prospect on a personal level and talk about what matters to them and the problems they face.

Be casual, yet compelling; start with your intentions and be real all through your pitch.

4. OWN YOUR CONVERSATION

Dialogue is paramount in consultative selling. Nevertheless, you determine the direction of the conversation, and your prospects need to understand that you are collaborating with them to solve their complex business problems.

You should prepare case studies and examples of related works you have completed in your client's niche with concise facts and details.

When you own the conversation, you are also demonstrating your credibility. It also enables you to shape your prospect's perceptions but is not a privilege to dominate. You should be creative with utilizing silence to drive home your points and let the prospects or clients share.

An instance where you can use silence is after making an offer; your silence can put some pressure on your prospects as they get to feel what's on the ground.

5. LEVERAGE FEEDBACK

Every bit of feedback counts - positive or constructive. When your client shares a concern or disagrees, they are communicating their requirements and sharing what they expect to make progress. Never take this personally.

It's important to take note of the feedback and do well to ask your clients if the solutions discussed align with their expectations. Asking your clients as such means you are committed to collaborating with them in the consultative sales process. In some other cases, it will also help you to expand your offering.

If you were selling endpoint security and a retail enterprise tells you they need to train their staff on how to protect themselves from ransomware, that alone can offer you insight on how to customize your pitch to cover these pain points in your sales process.

6. RESEARCH YOUR CLIENT REQUIRE-
MENTS AND SHARE RELEVANT INSIGHTS

Try to research your client's business and industry before you make the first call. This will afford you the requisite fundamental knowledge to ask insightful and incisive questions.

Also, research the possible gaps and problems beforehand to figure out the opportunities you can leverage to create unique value.

HOW TO APPLY CONSULTATIVE SELLING STRATEGY

1. INJECT INSIGHTS INTO QUESTIONS

2. DEVELOP KNOWLEDGE-BASED TRUST

3. KEEP YOUR COMMUNICATION CONVERSATIONAL REAL (BEING EMOTIONALLY VULNERABLE)

4. OWN YOUR CONVERSATION

5. LEVERAGE FEEDBACK

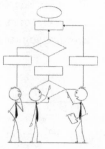

6. RESEARCH YOUR CLIENT REQUIREMENTS AND SHARE RELEVANT INSIGHTS

7. LISTEN

As a cybersecurity salesperson selling security solutions, you should familiarize and update yourself about regulations and standards related to your prospect's industry. That will help you to figure out how your product stands out in helping your clients achieve compliance with those regulations.

Once these ideas are clear, you can map your capabilities to align with your client's needs. Interestingly, your clients will buy into it as the information you are presenting is relatable.

It is imperative to stick to relevant and cogent ideas. Don't succumb to the urge to pour out all the outcomes of your research. Only use a few, yet concise insights to impact the conversation. If you know your client needs customized training for its team, highlight the facts and tailor the ideas from a consultative perspective.

7. LISTEN

Consultative selling is about the client. It means you have to prioritize their opinions. Allow them to talk but own the conversation, as I stated previously. Ownership differs from dominance. Don't interrupt their line of thought with what you perceive as solutions to their pain points. Take note of non-verbal cues that may convey what they might find difficult to communicate with words.

As a consultant, you need to sympathize with them and let them know your priority is getting their problems solved.

The sales landscape is dynamic, and the ability to build a formidable relationship with your clients goes a long way to provide you with an opportunity to upsell and cross-sell in the future. The consultative method gives you that leverage.

CHAPTER FOURTEEN

INBOUND SELLING - STRATEGIES FOR CYBERSECURITY SALESPEOPLE

So far, I have shared how you can deploy sales methodologies such as *Challenger Selling, Mahdi Selling, Solution Selling* and *Consultative Selling*.

The truth is that the sales environment is also embracing transformation, and right now, the information buyers need to make a purchasing decision is right at their fingertips. There is a power shift with the buyer having the upper edge in the buying and selling process. The information age has now allowed people to research and be equipped with everything about your product/service. They can tell you about your competition, reviews, and even pricing.

How then do you 'compete' with empowered clients if you are yet to transform your sales process? Regardless of what forms the basis of your sales process - targeted outreach or inbound leads, complex or straightforward sales process — you just can't underestimate the potential of inbound sales. This is because inbound sales reinvent your sales approach to align with today's empowered clients. This enables you to sell the way your client wants to buy.

WHAT ARE INBOUND SALES?

'Inbound' is a personalized and helpful sales methodology that allows salespeople to focus on the pain points and concerns. This sales methodology puts the salesperson in the position of a trusted consultant and enables them to align the process to fit the buyer's journey.

INBOUND VS. OUTBOUND SALES

Inbound selling aims to attract interested buyers to your products or service and build a solid relationship with them so they can succeed. Buyers coming in versus buyers you have to go out of your way to attract. With outbound sales, the tactic is to engage prospects whether they are interested in your offering or not.

Having understood how inbound selling differs from outbound sales, let's explore some proactive strategies you can leverage to sell the way your prospects want to buy.

INBOUND SALES TECHNIQUES

START WITH YOUR BUYER'S JOURNEY

Traditional salespeople construct a sales process that revolves around *their* needs and expectations – not the clients'. For them, it's about ticking the box to see if all parameters have been met without taking thought from their prospects or empowering them to own the purchasing process. This approach has disengaged buyers and delivers little or no value to them.

Here's the fact of the matter;

Your clients don't want to be prospected, pitched or closed. They are not deriving much value from most of these experiences as they can quickly get the same information from a YouTube channel, read some Quora answers or ask Alexa or Google.

Did you know that prospects detest salespeople generally? Now, most companies don't want to believe they are vulnerable to attacks until an incident occurs in the Cybersecurity world.

If you cannot add value beyond what your prospects can research online and independently (before a security incident), it is of no point engaging them at all.

Inbound selling is value-driven. It begins with the Buyer's journey. You already understand their world before you chat with them or call them.

Here's a framework you can use to demystify your Buyer's journey:

HOW TO UNDERSTAND YOUR BUYER'S JOURNEY

AWARENESS

This stage lets your clients figure out concerns or pain points they want to address.

Decide if you're going to prioritize.

You can reflect on these questions:

- *How do clients describe the goals or pain points your product addresses?*

- *How do they research further about these goals or pain points?*

- *How do they conclude whether the goal or pain point is prioritized?*

CONSIDERATION

Your client has already defined their pain points and has resolved to address them in this stage.

They review several methods or strategies to deal with their problems or achieve their goals.

You can reflect on these questions to understand your client's consideration phase:

- *What set of solutions are your clients reviewing?*

- *How do they perceive the advantages and the disadvantages of each set?*

- *What is your unique selling point?*

DECISION

Clients have decided on a solution category or set in this phase. They itemize vendors and offerings in the chosen category and select the best fit for their requirements.

To understand your client's decision stage, you can ask yourself these questions:

- *What solutions do your clients typically review?*

- *What parameters do they base their reviews on?*

- *What makes your solution stand out in the client's eyes?*

- *Who are the stakeholders in the decision-making, and how do their perspectives differ on the decision?*

This fictitious case study of AA Recruiting, a recruiting agency that helps tech companies source for developers and engineers, will enable us to put these three stages into context.

AA Recruiting has ten on-staff recruiters that form the team, excluding the CEO. Hilton's core business is to help tech companies outsource software developers and engineers.

The agency targets U.S-based tech companies that generate $100 million US in revenue.

On-staff recruiters find tech companies that fit their target personae and convince them to collaborate with them to help them source for developers.

The CEO of AA Recruiting decides to leverage the inbound sales method to power their client acquisition process.

DESIGN A SALES PROCESS THAT ALIGNS WITH THE CLIENT'S BUYER JOURNEY

Once you have defined the client's journey, the next thing is to develop your sales process. As you may recall, traditional sales processes build a sales process first, while inbound selling defines the client's journey before building a sales process. The alignment between you and your clients throughout the purchasing and selling period is the support that the inbound sales process offers to buyers.

Thus, to build a cybersecurity inbound sales process, ask what you should be doing throughout the awareness, consideration, and decision phases to support your clients. This four-phased framework can guide you in developing your inbound sales process:

- Inbound cybersecurity sales teams **IDENTIFY** prospects with pain points or concerns they can help with. These people eventually become leads.

- They **CONNECT** with these leads intending to assist them in deciding on prioritizing their pain points or leaving them. If the prospects decide to proceed, they become qualified leads.

- Next, they **EXPLORE** the pain points and goals to determine whether it fits their qualified leads' context. The qualified leads become opportunities if they are best-fits.

- Lastly, they **ADVISE** these opportunities based on the benefits their offering has in order to address the leads' concerns. If the prospect agrees your offering is the best fit at this stage, they become your clients.

Let's look at a hypothetical sales process of AA Recruiting, aligned with the buyer's journey.

CLIENT

Aware of recruiting challenges

Potential pain

- *Optimize hiring quality to deal with increasing attrition.*

- *Improve hiring pace to align with accelerated revenue goals.*

- *Decrease cost per hire by reeling in costs.*

Research best practices on Quora, eBooks and Blogs

- *Converse with peers in the same niche.*

Consider In-House Recruiter vs. External Agency

- *Compare in-house recruiters with an external agency.*

- *Design case to assess external recruiting agencies.*

- *Review different sets of recruiting agencies.*

Decide on External Recruitment Agency

- *Itemize the best-fit recruiting agencies.*

- *Design assessment parameters for recruiting agencies.*

- *Hold meetings with the agencies to evaluate fit.*

- *Decide on an agency.*

- *Negotiate and finalize a contract with the chosen firm.*

SALESPERSON

Identify Prospects with Recruiting Challenges.

- *Track inbound leads and agencies.*

- *Implement social selling.*

- *Figure out passive buyers on LinkedIn.*

- *Network at events.*

Connect with Identified Prospects

- *Share content (e.g. whitepapers, webinars, blogs on clients' recruiting challenges via email or voice note).*

- *Engage with clients on social media (LinkedIn or Clubhouse, for instance).*

- *Invite clients to attend consultation sessions on their recruitment problem areas.*

Explore Set of Solutions and Recruitment Agency Selection

- *Explore the most significant recruiting challenge and consider why*

- *Explore how clients perceive in-house recruiters versus external agencies.*

- *Explore their perception of an ideal recruiting agency that matches their needs.*

Advise on Recruiting Agency selection

- *Advise clients on structuring their recruiting concerns.*

- *Advise clients on in-house recruiters in contrast to external agencies relating to their context.*

- *Advise clients on assessment parameters that are unique to their context.*

- *Offer case studies and ROI studies that fit the client's context.*

- *Illustrate how AA Recruiting is the best option for their context.*

- *Negotiate and conclude on terms.*

DEFINE YOUR 'IDENTIFY' PHASE

Most traditional salespeople aren't aware of any active buyers in a purchasing journey. They just pick a few clients they feel are qualified and call them randomly.

Here's the issue: Most of these clients have already transitioned into the Awareness phase before reaching out to a salesperson. These active clients are the first set you target with your cybersecurity products. Go beyond the conventional and separate the passive clients from the active clients.

Inbound top sales performers focus on active buyers who have already moved to the Awareness phase. These buyers have checked your Linkedin/siberXchange page, subscribed to your emails, filled out forms or left traces of their needs in one way or the other.

IDEAL BUYER PROFILE

It is important to define which clients you can help and which you cannot. This is known as setting up a perfect client profile. The profile will enable you to determine who your ideal client is.

Once you have defined your ideal client profile, employ this hierarchy of lead sources to rank leads.

INBOUND LEADS: Web visitors who share their contact details through a conversion form and work in a firm or organization that matches your ideal client profile.

INBOUND COMPANIES: Anonymous web visitors from firms or organizations match your ideal client profile. In this situation, you don't have the client's contact details, but you have the corporate details. You can use CRM tools to identify those companies.

TRIGGER EVENTS: These are a type of event that reveals active buyers. Some hypothetical events could incorporate mentions of your social media handles or that of a competitor by the prospects, mentions of hashtags or keywords that match your value proposition, a blog article or social media post published by a prospect, or a new executive recruited by the company.

SOCIAL SELLING: Dedicate a few hours to publishing content each week, comment on relevant conversations and share content by industry experts that may interest your buyers. This will project your brand to clients and enable you to gain more leads you can pursue.

SHARED CONNECTIONS: These are passive prospects that match your ideal client profile and are connected to personal friends and families, colleagues or professional acquaintances.

PASSIVE BUYERS: Figure out passive buyers who match your ideal client profile as a last resort.

Whichever way you adopt, supply your identified leads with content that is centered around their demographics and interests.

DEFINE YOUR 'CONNECT' PROCESS

Traditional salespeople spend time and effort on cold voicemails and emails. This is the same generic elevator pitch that seeks to entice prospective clients to check a video or presentation about a product. If and when they succeed in getting on a call with a prospect, the rest of the effort is spent on qualifying prospects on their budget size and ability to spend it.

Clients in this digital age don't depend on insights from salespeople to learn about products and services. They can access the information they need on the internet. Also, the presentation bore them stiff at this phase of their journey. They want a two-way conversation with industry experts who can help them structure their pain points or goals.

If you're going to reach out to this set of modern prospects, you have to come up with customized information that fits into their context-interests, role, demography, and industry. Prepare an offer that aligns with the Awareness phase in your client's buying journey. It could be an eBook or a free consultation that provides the information clients are researching.

Inbound salespeople are also proactive at the Connect stage. They define their personas by segregating the market based on company type and highlighting specific targets in the different companies. Segmentation can be done by size, geographical location or industry. It can also be done by title, role, function or shared behaviours.

In our hypothetical example of AA Recruiting, the agency projects six personas:

PERSONA A: HR & Recruitment Director at a Cybersecurity Consulting company

PERSONA B: VP of Sales at a Space company

PERSONA C: CEO of a Technology company

PERSONA D: VP of Sales at an AI Company

PERSONA E: Director of Recruiting at a Technology Company

PERSONA F: CEO of a Cybersecurity company

With personas designed, you can outline your sequences or outreach strategies for each of the personas. A persona sequence outlines how to reach your client (social, email, phone, etc.), when and how often.

Lastly, you will need to design your outreach content for each task in the sequence. Ensure you customize the outreach to align with your client's context, which you already uncovered in the 'identity' stage.

DEFINE YOUR 'EXPLORE' PROCESS

Most traditional salespeople start presenting demos immediately after they notice some level of interest by prospects. Meanwhile, they don't fully know their prospective buyer's context to add value to the demo or pitch. Why? The buyer context is yet to fully develop, so salespeople who engage them to resort to a generic pitch or demo presentation, fielding information prospects already checked out on the internet.

Inbound cybersecurity sales performers go into an exploratory mode when buyers show interest. They understand they have not built a level of trust and rapport with their clients to generate a customized presentation. Sometimes, they don't even think they have what it takes to assist clients in this stage. What they do majorly is to develop trust and investigate the clients' objectives via exploratory communication.

They leverage their credibility and experience to navigate the pain points and concerns of the clients. Their expertise can evaluate whether they have what it takes to address their clients' concerns that clients can handle independently.

Inbound salespeople also guide their clients using strategic questioning and value proposition to help them generate conclusions as to whether the product is the best fit for their requirements.

If you want to think inbound, you can design an exploratory guide to inform an efficient discussion with your client.

DEFINE YOUR 'ADVICE' PROCESS

Traditional salespeople use the same case studies and presentations for all buyers. They may figure out some of their clients' concerns to know if they are interested before reverting to a generic presentation.

Meanwhile, clients have already seen the same content online in this digital age. They can just match the generic value proposition with their requirements, and where traditional salespeople are meant to help, they fail to make this connection happen.

Inbound salespeople are not like that. They tailor their presentation to the client's context using the data generated at the Connect phase. During the exploratory discussion, they investigated if the client can be assisted, needs help, or wants assistance.

Understanding the client's context and aligning the presentation accordingly, adds value to the client's journey beyond what clients can research online. They are the translators of generic value propositions available on the company's page, and their goal is to bring it down to the client's situation.

Cybersecurity salespeople need to evolve regardless of the sales methodologies they are using. You can keep using an obsolete technique to solve emerging challenges. It is time to transform your sales process.

Join me in the next chapter as we explore Sales Transformation.

CHAPTER FIFTEEN

HOW TO TRANSFORM YOUR CYBERSECURITY SALES APPROACH

"Two things define you: Your patience when you have nothing and your attitude when you have everything."

Ali ibn Abi Talib

Have you ever wondered why certain salespeople consistently exceed their quota while others lag behind schedule?

Why do some people experience ongoing sales success while others don't?

The simple, straightforward answer to that is "transformation of sales approach."

SALES PROCESS TRANSFORMATION

What does that mean, you ask?

The process of improving or modernizing a company's sales operations is known as 'sales transformation'. This shift is motivated by a company-wide desire to attain certain goals or objectives that are heavily influenced by the sales process, such as growing revenue.

So, why are there such disparities in people's sales success today? Is this because some salespeople are just more natural closers than others?

Yes, this could be the case. However, I believe there is something far more significant going on here. In truth, in my years of sales experience, I've observed something entirely different that I feel is at the core of sales success.

CONSIDER THE FOLLOWING FOUR BASIC SALES APPROACHES

i. Identifying a business opportunity

ii. Determining the needs of the customer

iii. Preparing a proposal, and

iv. Negotiating and closing the deal.

Traditional sales training focuses on negotiating and closure, and popular thinking says that sales success is equal to ABC (Always Be Closing). If you can double your closing rate, your sales will increase by 100%.

Is this achievable, and can it be done in a long-term manner? I don't believe so. So then, what is the real secret to today's sales success?

The answer is explained in the following sales transformation steps:

HOW TO TRANSFORM YOUR SALES APPROACH

STEP 1: 'YOU SHOULD BE AWARE OF WHERE YOU ARE AND WHERE YOU ARE HEADING'

Always make a convincing case for change. Define the issue you are attempting to tackle and why the existing situation is insufficient.

We agree with one caveat: your clear vision should be founded on data-driven insights rather than hunches.

Traditionally, a sales team rarely understands their commercial capabilities, according to research. A high-performing sales team, on the other hand conducts a systematic assessment of their capabilities at a granular level before making decisions.

The top-of-the-board sales performers are deliberate in assessing their strengths and weaknesses across all skills, then mapping them against their sales objectives to determine which capabilities to prioritize. Everyone in the team can identify which two to three sales competencies their team focuses on developing, how they're doing it, and how well the effort translates into impact.

Leading sales teams hold multi-day workshops to translate their initial vision into actual goals and timetables that can be filtered down from the executive team. Tremendous energy is released to begin the transition when a visionary aim is linked to a clear and practical timeline.

STEP 2: ASSEMBLE A TRANSFORMATION TEAM

The next step is to build a resilient sales transformation team based on the objectives and facts that have been established. It should comprise marketing, sales, operations, and business-unit leaders and is often led by the CEO, the head of sales, the chief marketing officer, or even the chief operating officer.

Team members must be respected, and their co-workers must believe they can't afford to lose them. HR and communications professionals should also be included, as well as a project manager who keeps everyone focused on the next phase of the trip and keeps track of the appropriate metrics.

Because sales changes are lengthy processes including risk, the team must develop deep levels of trust to maintain strong morale over time. Learning what makes each person tick, understanding motivations, and determining attitudes toward change and risk should be part of the trust-building process.

What matters is that team members are aware of their own and their colleagues' motives as they embark on a transformational path filled with new experiences and hazards.

STEP 3: PROSPECTING OR IDENTIFYING AN OPPORTUNITY

You may drastically improve your sales success by just locating additional prospects. You'll double the number of sales you make if you double the number of prospects while keeping your closing rate equal.

So ABP (Always be Prospecting) is the key to sales success.

In prospecting, conventional wisdom dictates that you employ usual methods, such as newspapers, magazines, journals, periodicals, reviews, and newsletters.

Traditional tactics, in my experience, offer relatively conventional results, which are frequently insufficient to alter your sales success today.

Here's a quick and easy strategy that is incredibly effective. It's simple to do, inexpensive, and effective. Try it and see how many qualified prospects you can find for a three-hour investment of your time.

Take part in as many of these activities as you can. Industry events for or related to your target consumers' businesses are a gold mine for a prospector. Simply spend time there conversing with others. Talk to as many people as you can. From conference participants to coffee break conversationalists to conference speakers and panelists, there is something for everyone. As a founder of a cybersecurity event company, the number of stories and testimonials I have seen and heard about, I can say this is the motherload of gold mines.

Talk to exhibitors in their booths and people you encounter on the exhibition floor at trade shows and exhibitions. Learn about their industry, significant industry players, sales arguments, positioning, and, whenever feasible, learn their PAIN points from them. You'll take a Rolodex full of business cards home with you. The Exhibitor Catalogue is the bible for prospectors.

STEP 4: NETWORKING

To transform your sales approach, you must meet as many people as possible, have a clear goal in mind for each encounter, and believe in the "n + 1" philosophy. That is, you should never anticipate speaking with someone who is a direct prospect for your products or services, but you can be sure that person will know someone who is.

And it is to this individual that you wish to communicate, meet, and finally, make your proposal.

HOW CAN YOU IMPROVE YOUR NETWORKING SKILLS?

I recommend joining one or two networking organizations, such as business groups or business luncheons, business clubs, associations, special interest groups, Toastmasters International, or school or university alumni groups. siberX has built a fantastic cybersecurity platform that allows thousands of people to connect—sending messages or tagging them on the wallboard.

Second, create a meeting participant file and keep it updated regularly.

Third, make an effort to keep your network alive by keeping in touch regularly and expanding it with new contacts.

Consider how you can add value to your contacts by considering how you may assist them.

The mindset for networking success is 'give before you gain.' Over time, your efforts will be amply rewarded.

Last but not least, make it a habit. Prospecting is, in fact, purposeful networking.

STEP 5: WEB-BASED NETWORKING

Today, we all have access to many web-based solid tools for locating opportunities and prospects. You can use web search tools with pinpoint accuracy to find new possibilities.

You can also conduct a Linkedin/siberXchange search of all founders or CEOs/CISOs/CIOs based in Canada and rank them according to the number of persons in their networks. This will help you learn about people who have the largest personal networks since they can introduce you to prospective clients ('n+1 thinking').

Being a prospecting machine has never been easier with buddies you'd meet in this manner.

STEP 6: PUBLIC SPEAKING

Make speeches and other public appearances to generate leads. This necessitates being an expert in your chosen field. It's not as difficult as you may assume. Choose any topic on Cybersecurity; showcase your knowledge and passion. Go live on platforms such as Zoom, Linkedin or siberXchange.

Then take advantage of any opportunity to speak to a group, give a presentation on your topic, be a panelist, or engage in a discussion group. It's all about high visibility exposure, precisely what you want. siberX and many other organizations host many events, and this is a great place to start.

People will approach you and share their business cards or eCards with you. This is the epitome of reverse psychology. You are no longer the same person after speaking to a group. You've been changed into an expert, a guru, and you've gained superhuman abilities.

Everyone wants to meet you, chat you up, and obtain your business card due to this. Take as much as you can. Instead of pushing, use this approach to create pull. As a result, stack the deck in your favour. People will be genuinely expecting that you will contact them due to your brief business card exchange.

STEP 7: MAKE THE MOST OF YOUR CLIENT'S SUPPLY CHAIN

Prospecting among your client's consumers, suppliers, partners, or competitors is the goal. Always be on the lookout for sales opportunities in your client's "company ecosystem."

Let me show you three simple ways to accomplish this:

i. *Customers of your client:* One of your clients provides services to the maritime shipping business. You'd like to sell your cybersecurity software and services to their clients to help manage the security of their maritime transactions. Request that your client introduces you to three of their most crucial maritime shipping clients.

ii. *Client's Vendors:* Another of your customers has PCs from a well-known company. Your cybersecurity software functions most cost-effectively and reliably on particular combinations of that hardware manufacturer's equipment. Request an introduction from your client to the hardware vendor, and then pitch your product to the hardware vendor's channel partners as a turn-key solution to suit their customers' online security requirements.

iii. *Competitors of the Client:* Prospecting your client's competitors is also a great idea. They frequently have the same or comparable company difficulties, and you have first-hand knowledge of how your solution aids in the resolution of these issues. You have a reference customer who is a respected rival and an established supplier in their industry. If you navigate your client's supply chain, you'll find a gold mine of prospecting chances for your products and services.

STEP 8: MAKE USE OF JOURNALISTS' EXTENSIVE NETWORK OF CONTACTS AND INDUSTRY KNOWLEDGE

Journalists have many connections and are informed about various topics relevant to you and your company. They have a high-level view of what is going on in your sector and are always in touch with many influential people. The kind of important people you'd like to know!

Because journalists speak with industry executives, thought leaders in your field, competitors, and even customers, you should get to know them and make them part of your "virtual team." Conduct an interview with a journalist. Yes, employ deviant thinking and the reversal of traditional roles. How?

Invite a journalist to speak on a panel at a conference you're arranging. Request that they overview the industry or talk about future trends or issues your industry faces. Why?

i. *They are seen as an independent thought leader, which offers you credibility.*

ii. *They will subsequently tell others about you and your company. Encourage them to talk about you and your company.*

iii. *Invite or fund a journalist to moderate a consumer event or an industry conference.*

iv. *Alternatively, inquire about current consumer issues and available solutions.*

Alternatively, you can also request that they offer a specific case study. The journalist's presentation and remarks will be associated with you and your solution.

STEP 9: MAKING USE OF REFERRALS

The most effective technique to approach someone you don't know is through someone they know. Using a 'referral' is a term for this type of strategy. A good reference provides you with exclusive access to a receptive audience.

When you contact someone through a referral, you automatically have the same trust and respect as the person who referred you. Make the most of this when describing or presenting your concept. The amount and quality of referrals you may create are strongly related to your sales success.

How do you get people to refer to you? You simply ask for them. Everyone you meet is eager to provide you with referrals if you only ask. How you ask, the amount and quality of references you receive are determined by how you ask.

Here's an easy example: *"Can you identify 2-3 colleagues of yours who may have the same requirements or problems as you?"* at the end of your next client appointment. Then, when you contact them, ask if you can include their name in the conversation. Also, make a list of each referral's name, title, firm, phone number, and email address. Double-check that you can use your contact's name and make a reference to your conversation.

Consider the following scenario:

"Hello, Mr. Smith, Lynda James of 123 Ltd. gave me your name and urged that I contact you. Mary and my company are working together to prevent online fraud and cyber-attacks. She thought you might be interested in the great results she's seen in her five main city stores utilizing our ABC cybersecurity technology."

You will captivate your prospect's full and undivided attention with an opening introduction like this, and doors will immediately open at all levels of your prospect's organization.

STEP 10: TAKE ADVANTAGE OF SPORTING AND CORPORATE EVENTS

At events, there are a lot of new opportunities, from school sports gatherings to corporate VIP hospitality events. Attend some local sporting activities where you can meet other people with similar sporting interests or go to your child's school sports events where you can meet other parents, and then use "n+1" thinking and ask for references to find new prospects.

HOW TO TRANSFORM YOUR
SALES APPROACH

STEP 1: 'YOU SHOULD BE AWARE
OF WHERE YOU ARE AND
WHERE YOU ARE HEADING'

STEP 2: ASSEMBLE A
TRANSFORMATION TEAM

STEP 3: PROSPECTING OR
IDENTIFYING AN OPPORTUNITY

STEP 4: NETWORKING

STEP 5: WEB-BASED
NETWORKING

STEP 6: PUBLIC SPEAKING

VIP Hospitality Events for Business: These events are an excellent way to invite those prospects that are difficult to reach. When you're trying to meet with senior management, you'll often find them busy and challenging to achieve. These are the folks who make the final decisions.

George has some valuable advice on this, he mentions that, in advance of hosting these prospects, a vital consideration is having intentional strategies prepared for each known invitee. Your tactical goals will likely change as each client relationship and organization are different, so it is essential to consider what you are trying to achieve out of each interaction specifically.

The goal is to make the event so alluring and the invitation so distinguished that potential attendees will go to any length to attend. The International Tennis Grand Slam, such as Roland Garros or Wimbledon, the Formula One Grand Prix, the UEFA Cup, or the Rugby World Cup, are all examples.

Now, make every effort to invite as many VIP prospects and customers as possible. Existing customers can talk about their experiences working with you and your firm and provide "spontaneous testimonials" to the VIP prospects you've invited.

Give your prospects a VIP invitation to a high-profile event, and you'll be remembered for the rest of their lives. You've established reciprocity for later usage, even if they can't make it or decline your invitation.

STEP 11: "DO NOT EAT ALONE"

This has to be one of the most effective and enjoyable methods of prospecting that I am aware of, but it's also one of the least employed. This is the most straightforward approach to having "privileged talks" where essential information and ideas are exchanged.

When people are calm and enjoying a good meal, I have discovered that they are more open, honest, and straightforward with you. They are happy, and they are fulfilled. Make inquiries about them. The key to being a good conversationalist and getting others to open up is to let them speak more than you.

Get to know them. Give them opportunities to share parts of their lives with you. Ask questions and be sincere with your inquisitive vibe.

Get a little personal by means of asking them about their families, interests, travels, and perspectives. Your genuine interest will be rewarded with knowledge rich in truth, opinion, emotion, and the opportunity

HOW TO TRANSFORM YOUR
SALES APPROACH

STEP 7: MAKE THE MOST OF YOUR CLIENT'S SUPPLY CHAIN

STEP 8: MAKE USE OF JOURNALISTS' EXTENSIVE NETWORK OF CONTACTS AND INDUSTRY KNOWLEDGE

STEP 9: MAKING USE OF REFERRALS

STEP 10: TAKE ADVANTAGE OF SPORTING AND CORPORATE EVENTS

STEP 11: "DO NOT EAT ALONE"

STEP 12: MONITOR YOUR PROGRESS OVER TIME

for prospecting. Make them a part of your network by establishing a long-term relationship with them that you may revisit in the future.

Learn about the industry and the market. Inquire about their knowledge of market trends, industries, sectors, consumers, projects, and individuals in your areas of interest. Inquire about their coworkers, associates, and acquaintances to see whether they know anyone who shares their interests, concerns, or issues.

Always aim to acquire three referrals before going out to coffee. If you do it well, you'll walk away with the equivalent of thousands of dollars in industry knowledge and market data and three referrals and a lifelong friend for the price of a $50 lunch. That has to be the best return on investment I've ever seen! Assume that most people eat three meals daily and work five days per week.

That gives you 15 chances to eat with someone new each week. Set a weekly target of two lunch meetings, one breakfast meeting, and one evening meeting. This is probably my favourite way to meal plan! Now is the time to start preparing your schedule!

STEP 12: MONITOR YOUR PROGRESS OVER TIME

Monitoring the achievement of your sales transformation goals over time, like with any sales process, gives you insight into what is working and helps you discover issue areas before you fall short of your overall goals.

If your aim at the start of the transformation process was to increase revenue by 7% by the end of the year, this is unlikely to happen all at once. If you've created Objectives and Key Results (OKRs), you've probably discovered that there are a variety of tasks you and your sales team will need to follow to achieve these objectives. The ability to track progress over time provides insight into how your entire team reacts to the new changes, allowing you to update or change processes as needed.

It's also easy to emphasize early accomplishments to motivate your team when tracking development over time. Sales transformations can be challenging for salespeople because their day-to-day activities may alter significantly. Seeing that their efforts have paid off can encourage them to stick with the new plan.

CHAPTER SIXTEEN

HOW TO BUILD A CYBERSECURITY SALES PIPELINE

I f you spend any time in sales industry circles, you'll be exposed to the common topic of 'getting prospects into the pipeline,' 'growing your pipeline,' and 'filling your pipeline with hot 'leads', and you start to wonder, "what does a sales "pipeline" mean?

WHAT IS A SALES PIPELINE?

A sales pipeline is a series of steps that a prospect goes through as they transition from being a new lead to becoming a customer. The prospect is forwarded to the next stage after each pipeline stage is completed.

Though a sales pipeline's structure varies from firm to company, here are some more common stages:

1. QUALIFICATION:

The sales representative asks inquiries to see if the prospect has the need, budget, and authorization to purchase shortly.

2. MEETING:

The sales representative and the prospect debate the best solution for the prospect's demands.

3. PROPOSAL:

The sales representative delivers the prospect a precise quote that details what will be given, at what cost, and for how long.

4. CLOSING:

Contracts are signed after final talks. The prospect has now been converted into a paying customer.

HOW TO BUILD A CYBERSECURITY SALES PIPELINE?

Many salespeople and firms never create a sales pipeline that produces the outcomes they need to succeed. These are some tips for putting together a good cybersecurity sales pipeline. As explained earlier, any list of *"qualified prospects that aren't ready to buy right now"* is what we refer to as a "sales pipeline." "Fruit on a tree that hasn't matured" is a better analogy.

Now, you may have identified these leads as good customer prospects. You must, however, be available when these prospects are ready to buy. These prospect opportunities will wither away if you don't develop a contact pipeline for them. What's worse is when the prospect matures, someone else will be around, and you will miss out on new business.

The following steps would help you build a sales pipeline that closes deals:

STEP 1: RESEARCH YOUR TARGET MARKET.

What is the demographic of your target market? Even if your cybersecurity solution caters to a vast audience, there are certain characteristics they all share. Work to identify that *"shared, binding factor."*

It's critical to look beyond typical demographics, such as thirty-year-old tech workers earning between $50 and $100K per year. Learn about your audience's difficulties and pain spots to see how you may assist them.

Your sales pipeline will be easier to complete and more productive if you understand what motivates your audience to take each stage.

Here's the problem: Many businesses believe they know their target market. They do, however, rely on intuition rather than data. A huge blunder!

So, where do you look for information? Here are a couple of places to begin:

Enable the Demographics and Interests report in Google Analytics and utilize the data to figure out who visits your site.

CUSTOMER SERVICE REPRESENTATIVES: What are the issues that customers face? What are they searching for in terms of solutions? Customer service representatives interact with consumers daily and can supply information that you won't find anywhere else.

CUSTOMER SURVEYS: Conduct an annual survey to learn more about your customers and the difficulties they confront. This can aid sales activities and give data for product development.

Facebook, Instagram, LinkedIn, siberXchange and most other social media networks provide audience insights such as demographics and interests.

Knowing the answers to these questions will make it easier for you to identify your target audience, successfully address their problems, and distinctively position your brand.

STEP 2: CREATE BUYER PERSONAS FOR YOUR TYPICAL 'CLIENTELE'

You got a lot of data from Step 1, but what does that data mean? What effect will it have on your sales pipeline? Your audience research is relegated to spreadsheets without a buyer persona, which isn't very useful when selecting what landing page design to employ or what blog post to write.

You may create a buyer persona that embodies these features based on your customers' desire for your product and its use. Assume that a section of your audience consists of freelance-working mothers in their thirties who want to spend as little time as possible earning money online without worrying about losing their earnings to cyber-frauds.

Your buyer persona may be a fictional woman named Ava, 28, a mother of one who works as a freelance virtual assistant for a financial institution to give them a more personalized and engaging experience. You'll be able to create a complete sales journey for her after that. Is she familiar with your product or service because she learned about it on siberX, Facebook, LinkedIn, or industry events?

What data does she require to make a buying decision? Before making a purchase, who else will she consult? Is she the one who makes the final decision? What kind of media is she likely to consume the most? The responses to these questions will guide each phase of your sales pipeline.

Make a buyer persona for each major segment of your audience and use it to drive your decisions.

STEP 3: TRACK DOWN THOSE LEADS.

You have a good idea of who your target market is. You know what motivates them, and you've created a buyer profile to use as a barometer for your sales funnel. It's now time to start generating leads. There is no one-size-fits-all approach to generating leads; instead, consider your sector and target audience.

If your target demographic spends much time researching LinkedIn, for example, that could be the way to go.

Here are some alternative methods for generating leads:

- Offer a downloadable guide, eBook, template, or worksheets as a lead magnet to entice potential buyers.

- As a guest blogger, contribute to industry websites: Share your knowledge on well-known industry websites. Prospects will learn to trust you and are more likely to act on your advice.

- Make a free tool available: Is it possible to offer a free tool (or a limited-time free plan) to solve a problem that your target audience is experiencing? For example, MailChimp's email has a free limited subscription. Customers can test the program before making a purchase.

- Traffic to your website: Who comes to your site but does not leave their contact information? Track and identify anonymous site users so that they can be **targeted.**

Don't underestimate or overlook organic search traffic; improve your site so that individuals searching for "cybersecurity" can reach you.

STEP 4: DETERMINE WHICH LEADS ARE QUALIFIED AND WHICH ARE NOT

You should have a decent list of leads in your target audience at this point. However, there is a problem; not all leads are ready to purchase. Some people may still be in the awareness stage, while others may be evaluating their alternatives but not quite ready to buy.

The issue is that if you send all of your leads to sales at this point, you will waste much time chasing down leads who aren't ready to buy. Rather than upsetting your sales team, make sure to qualify leads and segregate those who aren't yet ready to convert.

However, there are a few signs to know when you are ready to convert:

- *They've looked over several pages on your site, including the pricing and services pages.*

- *A lead magnet has been downloaded/signed up for.*

- *They're looking through comparative pages.*

Leads ready to buy should be contacted immediately, while the rest should proceed to the engagement stage.

STEP 5: CREATE A SOCIAL MEDIA PRESENCE

Social media is a fantastic tool for meeting and interacting with new individuals before realizing they might need your services. It makes it simpler to identify your target audience and redirect them to your website. If you don't know how to run a social media campaign, you can hire a lead-generating agency specializing in social media marketing or reach out to siberX.

Using social media for B2B lead creation may seem strange, but siberXchange, Facebook, Twitter, and LinkedIn have tremendous reach. Even in B2B, giveaways and webinars can generate great outstanding leads. George Al-Koura shares valuable insight:

> *"Thought leadership can also play a critical factor in building a powerful and wide-reaching social media presence with a relatively low level of effort. By keeping a finger on the pulse of cutting-edge developments or current events, you can use your social media platforms to provide your audience free value by giving them a contextually personalized perspective on the issue you are speaking to.*
>
> *In becoming a trusted voice on industry-related issues, your ability to open sales discussions with your audience members becomes dramatically easier as your influencer clout will allow your reputation to emotionally 'open doors' for you before you even attempt to engage directly."*

STEP 6: INCREASE PARTICIPATION

Now is the ideal and perfect opportunity to connect and engage with your pipeline leads, and content reigns supreme at this stage. Anything entertaining for your customers, such as video lessons, reviews, guidelines, valuable blog pieces, case studies, and infographics would be worth considering. The idea is to regularly create helpful, exciting material and promote it on social media and other platforms to reach a bigger audience.

You should already know the best kind of content to use (from your research stage). Now go ahead and create that material, share it, and don't forget to use A/B testing to see which content and format your audience prefers.

STEP 7: CONVERT THEM

Your target market is well-informed and has established a strong interest in your cybersecurity product or service. They simply need one more nudge in the right direction. You've put in the majority of the effort, but you don't want to lose the deal now. Here are a few techniques to ensure that your efforts are rewarded:

Keep it simple on your sales page:

i.   Remove any clutter that may cause your customer to become distracted. There should be no more than three main elements in the ideal scenario.

ii.   Make a personalized video to wrap up the benefits or offer, demonstrating that your sales team is paying attention to what the prospects need.

iii.   Experiment with A Call to Action: Offer a checkout button (Buy now/Subscribe/Choose a plan), and learn more/start a trial/sign up for free/claim a discount, CTA for customers who are still unsure so you can follow up later.

iv.   Make it simple to convert: Don't make them fill out a 25-page form to get started; instead, keep pricing transparent. Make it as simple as possible for them to fork over their hard-earned money.

STEP 8: CREATE A SCALABLE SALES PIPELINE

You've done it! You should have at least a few clients by now – well done. You must ensure that you can repeat this procedure indefinitely to keep new leads pouring in.

Begin by putting each phase of the sales funnel to the test. You might discover that prospects you previously dismissed as unqualified simply require a little more education to convert.

Consider automating time-consuming operations like data input, email follow-ups, and lead distribution to your sales force. This will allow sales and marketing to devote more attention to strategy.

Also, don't forget to stay in touch with existing customers — ask for comments, give them a discount voucher for their next purchase, or simply say "thank you" for choosing your business.

Every master gardener plans the piping for a lawn or garden watering system down to the inch. They begin by drawing a plan of where the water should flow. The same is true in sales, only that instead of water, it will be your leads who feed sales. For maximum yield, the sales pipeline must be laid out so that it gives contact nourishment. This would be your best cybersecurity pipeline-selling practice.

If fruit trees could talk, they'd advise you not to forget about them and water them regularly. You should water the tree during the warmest months, just as you should contact your promising/prospective clients when they are most likely to require your services. This necessitates a system that controls your interactions with each client. The most crucial thing is to pay attention to your clients and adhere to industry-standard practices.

If a client says they'll be ready in six months, you should have a plan to keep in touch with them frequently. The most significant sales will come from sticking to your action strategy. Your sales plan, like an autonomous irrigation system, should be automated.

Although most businesses are distinct from one another, they all require a pipeline infrastructure. When creating your sales funnel, make sure it's tailored to your company's needs and flexible enough to change.

Consider this work in the same way as a garden plot or a fruit orchard. You'll want to make sure you're delivering the proper amount of water. This would be the appropriate sequence of sales contacts, such as email, lead magnet eBooks, follow-up messages, and phone conversations.

HOW TO FIX A LEAKY SALES PIPELINE?

Leaky Sales Pipeline? What is it? How do you fix this?

Is there a leak in your sales pipeline? **Answering 'no' can lead you to a bigger problem.**

To some extent, every company's sales pipeline leaks. The question is, have you done everything you can to keep it from leaking too much? Do you even have a picture of your sales pipeline?

As we've discussed earlier, a Sales Pipeline begins with an initial inquiry and concludes with a transaction. While each company's Sales Pipeline is unique, there are certain commonalities.

There is a necessity to create queries in any firm. Advertising, cold calling, public relations, and word of mouth are suitable options. This could be a phone call in response to an advertisement. In retail, a customer may stroll in the door after being drawn in by your blog posts and social media contents or your siberXchange/LinkedIn/Facebook/Twitter ads.

HOW TO BUILD A CYBERSECURITY SALES PIPELINE?

STEP 1: RESEARCH YOUR TARGET MARKET.

STEP 2: CREATE BUYER PERSONAS FOR YOUR TYPICAL "CLIENTELE"

STEP 3: TRACK DOWN THOSE LEADS

STEP 4: DETERMINE WHICH LEADS ARE QUALIFIED AND WHICH ARE NOT.

HOW TO BUILD A CYBERSECURITY SALES PIPELINE?

STEP 5: CREATE A SOCIAL MEDIA PRESENCE

STEP 6: INCREASE PARTICIPATION

STEP 7: CONVERT THEM

STEP 8: CREATE A SCALABLE SALES PIPELINE

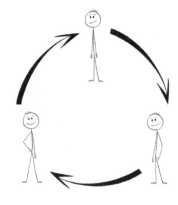

George highlights some important advice. "An important component to consider if a cold approach is used as a lead generating method is not merely 'cut and paste' an email or message script and send it to a random executive or organizational entry point. Adding some customized personalization to a cold contact message will vastly improve the odds for the success of that approach. By personalizing the message, the recipient will factor their feelings about you and your message; it will.".

This is the initial phase in any company's sales pipeline. However, from the time an inquiry is received until the time a transaction is made, several procedures are frequently involved. Closing the deal would be the final stage in this primary Sales Pipeline.

Every business owner should be aware of their Sales Pipeline and where it leaks. What proportion of enquirers consent to an initial appointment using the generic pipeline above? How many of them are willing to accept a formal proposal or request a quote?

Finally, what percentage of those who receive a formal proposal or quote convert to sales? You can monitor the performance of moving prospects down the pipeline and see where your sales process needs to be improved by understanding each phase in your Sales Pipeline.

There is no such thing as a leak-proof sales pipeline. In reality, there are some folks you would rather not have as customers. They could be bargain seekers, time wasters, or folks with a bad credit history. As a result, you should have a screening mechanism to weed out people who aren't qualified to be your consumers.

To be effective, this screening procedure should identify unqualified prospects early in the pipeline before you invest too much time with them. However, if you're turning away many unqualified leads, you should reconsider your lead creation strategy.

On the other hand, all other prospects are qualified by definition. You want to keep your loss to a minimum. If there is a significant loss in receiving that initial appointment, perhaps a script for staff to turn that initial inquiry into a meeting should be devised. Sales training on establishing rapport and need, creating desire, and producing value should be addressed if the losses in getting a request for a proposal or quotation are significant. If proposals (or quotes) have a low acceptance rate, there could be an issue with the offer or the salesperson's closing technique.

Set up tracking systems to track how prospects go through your sales pipeline. Analyze the losses at each stage of the process. You'll be able to see what you're doing right and where your pipeline is leaking if you understand your sales pipeline. Then you may begin fixing those leaks!

CHAPTER SEVENTEEN

UNDERSTANDING & AVOIDING THE CYBERSECURITY SALES PITFALLS

To be a great cybersecurity salesperson takes both talent and skill.

To perfect the sales process, you must practice, take risks, make mistakes, and learn from them, just as you would in sports.

There are a few basic blunders that practically every salesperson makes at some point in their career. Salespeople often exaggerate, overestimate, misread, and generally miss the mark when trying to close a deal.

To make your path to a perfect sale a little smoother, it's advisable to avoid some common cybersecurity sales pitfalls, including;

TOO MUCH TALKING AND NOT ENOUGH LISTENING

"To activate your faculty of inner wisdom, you must skillfully commit to establishing the self-discipline required for authentic listening."

Mahdi Raza

When you're attempting to sell your cybersecurity software/service, your natural tendency is to talk a lot: whether it is passionately highlighting the benefits and features of the product, bragging about your knowledge, and you know, you just keep on pushing, and pushing, and pushing.

This isn't effective because pushy cybersecurity salespeople rarely succeed. And let's face it, you're not the only one who sells this product! You would not want to purchase from a pushy salesperson either. It is a negative experience and often irritating.

Listen and engage in more open-ended inquiries instead. A 60/40 listening-to-talking ratio is ideal. It is a given that companies in practically every industry, from Wall Street to Main Street, whether large or little, are exposed to attacks. Theft of credit card data or personally identifiable information, on the other hand, frequently makes the news headlines.

As a result, businesses that don't handle this type of data often assume they aren't a viable target for cybercriminals.

In truth, enemies are launching large campaigns to access networks and infiltrate information systems and assets in every economic sector.

Organizations have valuable knowledge and a reputation to protect. Every company must know this reality and try to detect and prevent the potentially catastrophic damage that cyber-attacks can wreak.

What if the company's network was irreparably destroyed for a few weeks? What if wages couldn't be paid, customer communication was halted, or product websites were shut down? What if a hacker was able to compromise a company's most critical infrastructure? Adversaries are increasingly deploying digital attacks to destroy critical assets and steal data physically.

You can better grasp the customer's business needs and personalize your service by listening more and asking focused questions like the ones highlighted above. It will also show that you care by allowing you to get to know them as individuals (as well as their preferences and tastes).

Want to see the cherry on top? By asking questions and listening, you allow the potential customer to do all of the legwork for you, revealing their primary problem points and identifying solutions. This is especially useful during the prospecting stage of the sales process (consideration and qualification).

FOCUSING ON THE PROBLEM RATHER THAN THE SOLUTION

"The problem is not the problem. The problem is your attitude towards the problem, and if you can see the problem as a door, you may just find gold."

Mahdi Raza

This is an old tip, but it is most likely the most significant. As a cybersecurity solutions firm, it is only natural that you'd be tempted to brag about all the unique qualities that your products and solutions have. But there's a slight problem with that approach — *sadly, it's not going to sell.*

Instead of explaining the features and benefits of your cybersecurity products, concentrate on how your cybersecurity solution can help your prospective clients solve their most pressing issues.

The solution you provide here is a simple and evident benefit that will entice your prospects to purchase! It's critical to remember that your prospective cybersecurity clients aren't as interested in *how* you do things as they are in *what* you can do.

I'm trying to convey that your cybersecurity product's features inform your prospects, but the benefits persuade them to buy!

GIVING AWAY TOO MUCH FOR NOTHING

"Always keep a little bit for yourself. If you pour out everything, there will be nothing left to move forward."

Mahdi Raza

This is a direct result of talking excessively. To gain the customer/clientele, some cybersecurity solutions/products firms give too much support for free, effectively turning themselves into unpaid cybersecurity consultants.

Of course, being helpful is a benefit. However, there must be boundaries.

Cybersecurity prospects especially love to hound cybersecurity products and services sales personnel for information and assistance; even if they have no intention of making a purchase, always remember that knowledge is power!

You may give away way too much information in your endeavour to capture the prospective client's heart without receiving anything in return. Instead of providing free cybersecurity consultations, provide "your product-relative" answers to cybersecurity problems and everyday issues as part of your sales pitch.

PUTTING A PREMIUM ON PRICE RATHER THAN VALUE

"If it doesn't add value, it's wasted."

Henry Ford

Always remember: *Value, not price, is what people buy.* You're stuck in denial if you think the price will sell the product. That is a dream that will not come true; now is the time to wake up.

For starters, relying mainly on low costs, offering discounts here and there, and offering special promotions would only provide you with short-term joy in the form of bargain hunters. This customer will buy from you but will leave as soon as someone else offers them a better deal.

Second, although the price is usually a deciding factor, most buyers seeking lower costs will not buy a product simply because it is inexpensive. They will purchase a product that is beneficial to them. If the value is significant, customers won't mind being charged more. Think about the concept of private schools, for example. This is a very lucrative business and many private schools, despite the costly tuition, have waiting lists for enrollment.

Interestingly, the private school demographic does not consist of society's elite. Many private school patrons are simple working-class families who see and accept the value in the private school system despite the costs versus publicly funded education.

Remind your prospective clients that buying cheap does not always equate to the best solution. Leading with value, not cost, is the way to go. Investing in higher-quality items will provide them with the value they deserve and reduce costs in the long run.

MAKING PROMISES YOU WON'T BE ABLE TO KEEP

"In looking for people to hire, look for three things: integrity, intelligence and energy. And if they don't have the first, the other two will kill you."

Warren Buffet

Overpromising and underperforming in business are the same as lying. Lying is a horrible way to start any relationship, regardless of how much you want to sell. Exaggerating the capabilities of your cybersecurity product or service, or even worse, concealing certain restrictions or specific conditions, will not get you very far. George Al-Koura adds to this;

Circling back to authenticity, this is where knowing your products, services and solutions to the degree that you can informally speak to them with confidence becomes paramount. Decision-makers in the industry pride themselves on sniffing out the snake oil sales pros and their offerings. Their ability to do so speaks to their reputations of rooting and avoid risk spending, typically upping their level of clout with their respective board of senior leadership. You might have the greatest offering in the world, but if you can't speak to it from a place of confidence that breeds trust with your customers, your engagement will go nowhere fast.

ASK YOURSELF, WOULD YOU SPEND MONEY ON LIES?

Allow the prospects to sell themselves instead of over-promising what you cannot deliver. You may achieve this by gently nudging the prospective clients in the correct direction with the right questions. Finally, they'll persuade themselves that they require your products or services.

Another option is to offer a free trial period, which can provide an opportunity for them to test out your cybersecurity solution. You can under-promise here and overdeliver to ensure that your prospects are pleasantly satisfied. If prospects have modest expectations, but the product can genuinely accomplish more, they will be blown away by the experience. This will aid you in persuading them to buy during the next step of the sale.

Overall, it's preferable to sell nothing than to sell something dishonestly. When your customers find out later that you "failed to mention" a problem, you will lose the customer, and your reputation and future purchases and referrals will be out of the equation.

HAVING NO INTENTION OF COMPLETING A SALE

"You don't have to get down on one knee, but you do have to pop the question!"

Hina Ali

You'd be shocked at how many excellent cybersecurity sales firms are selling just to create distinctive sales pitches and killer slideshows rather than selling. Their ordinary talents and a demonstration of their sales mastery keep them going, not the number of deals they've closed.

My advice is to hang your vanity at the door and enter a sale to convert the prospective client into a customer. You have to ask the prospect to buy — it's as simple as that! And the earlier you do it in the sales process, the better.

How? Declare confidently to the prospect that you want to close the sale right away. By adopting urgency, you won't let anything steal your sale. There isn't any other option.

NOT BEING PREPARED TO DEAL WITH OBJECTIONS

"I don't believe in failure. It is not a failure if you enjoyed the process."

Oprah Winfrey

Nobody enjoys hearing the word 'no.' However, allowing clients to say "no" does have advantages. This raises the value of saying "yes" when the time is appropriate. When buyers eventually see something they want, repeated rejections only strengthen their desire to buy.

I have successfully sold real estate for over 20 years, and this was one of the most common strategies I used. For example, I would make it a point to show the less desirable properties first, then save the best for last. It's a relief to say "Yes!" after saying "No!" for so long!

Dealing with sales objections is a true art. You must maintain your composure, demonstrate that you understand and appreciate their concerns, and respond honestly, respectfully, and clearly. When dealing with "annoying" issues, never use the phrase "as I previously stated." That's a passive-aggressive and sure-fire way to kill a vibe and a sale. Instead, accept the antagonistic question or criticism as a genuine point, rebut it, keep it light, and have fun.

Finally, if nothing else seems to be working, consider whether the prospect you're attempting to sell to is a suitable fit for you. A very crucial skill is the capacity to recognize and abandon a sale with a low closing chance. After all, statistics suggest that at least half of your prospects aren't a suitable fit for what you have to offer.

GETTING INTO AN ARGUMENT WITH A POTENTIAL CUSTOMER

"First learn the meaning of what you say, then speak."

Epictetus

Even though this may seem self-explanatory, believe it or not, many cybersecurity salespeople make this grave mistake. It's easy to lose your cool and start defending your truth when a prospect's concerns grow ridiculous or contradict logic. But don't do it. Not now. Not ever. Just don't.

You may lose the deal if you argue with potential customers. Almost all of the time. If you don't agree with what they're saying, either remain silent or say, "I can see where you're coming from." Ask questions to clarify their position, paraphrase or reflect on their statements, but never argue with them or present yourself combatively.

Again, if you feel like 'you're up against a brick wall,' it's best to move away and concentrate on other, more lucrative alternatives. You can't please everyone. Take what you can learn and move on.

UNDERSTANDING & AVOIDING THE CYBERSECURITY SALES PITFALLS

TOO MUCH TALKING AND
NOT ENOUGH LISTENING

FOCUSING ON THE PROBLEM
RATHER THAN THE SOLUTION

GIVING AWAY TOO MUCH
FOR NOTHING

PUTTING A PREMIUM ON
PRICE RATHER THAN VALUE

MAKING PROMISES YOU
WON'T BE ABLE TO KEEP

NOT BEING PREPARED

"He who fails to plan, plans to fail."

Sir Winston Churchill

You must prepare for the sale, just as you would for a job interview.

Learn everything you can about your prospective client. This is best achieved using a "buyer persona," which we talked about earlier.

Trust me; it will show if you go into a meeting with a potential consumer unprepared. Especially considering that your prospective clients have already scoured the internet for information on you! What if they are more familiar with you than you are with them?

Preparation will help you communicate more effectively and ask appropriate questions. Still, it will also allow you to tweak your offering, customize your sales pitch, and articulate the benefits of your cybersecurity solutions that will resonate with that specific prospective client and their firm.

To develop a solid rapport, research your prospective client's firm, professional and even personal background. Trust is built through rapport, and no one wants to buy something from someone they don't know. In the age of information and technology, choosing to know is choosing to remain ignorant. Remember, you are selling a digital product, and it is much more important to be on top of your knowledge game.

You must be prepared for anything and everything that may occur. That means having all of the facts you'll need to make your pitch and any additional documents your prospect may require. Becoming a valuable and trusted resource is essential to being a great salesperson. That entails anticipating the customer's wants and the logistical and interpersonal scenarios you might experience throughout your pitch.

UNDERSTANDING & AVOIDING THE CYBERSECURITY SALES PITFALLS

HAVING NO INTENTION OF COMPLETING A SALE

NOT BEING PREPARED TO DEAL WITH OBJECTIONS

GETTING INTO AN ARGUMENT WITH A POTENTIAL CUSTOMER

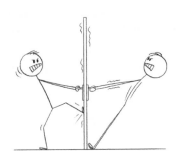

NOT BEING PREPARED

NOT BEING ABLE TO SPEAK WITH DECISION-MAKERS

NOT BEING ABLE TO SPEAK
WITH DECISION-MAKERS

*"To the world you may be one person, but to one person
you may be the world."*

Dr. Seuss

You can't sell to just anyone. You must deal with qualified people to make a purchasing choice to clinch a deal. Otherwise, you'll be squandering your time. Selling anything to just anyone is a waste of time that you should stop doing right now!

You're wasting your time and energy attempting to persuade someone or a company to buy your cybersecurity products, even if they don't need them. So, rather than selling to individuals who need your products or services and producing long-term value, you're selling to show that you can. Isn't that merely a display of self-importance?

Even if you manage to sell your cybersecurity product to a random person or firm, it will not be beneficial to your organization. Repeat clients, not one-time deals, are where the real money is made. Having loyal consumers pay you repeatedly is where you make money as a cybersecurity products firm, as existing customers account for 65% of a company's revenue, and repeat customers spend 33% more than new ones.

Selling your cybersecurity product to a corporation or firm that doesn't require it will never be a perfect match. They will, at the very least, be disappointed. Worst case scenario: they'll start talking to their partners, consumers, and others about your cybersecurity product's as ineffective and wasteful. As a result, your company's reputation may be associated with a "not-so-flattering" context on social media.

That is something you do not want. The bottom line is that you should never force a sale on someone who does not want or require your goods or services.

Get to know whom you're talking to. When calling on people, attempt to grasp their function and responsibilities inside the organization. Is this prospect a decision-maker? The answer to this question would influence your sales pitch.

Given that statements of top-line worth get decision-makers to respond well. Telling decision-makers about using your cybersecurity products or services to secure their increased revenue and profitability while losing none to cyber-attacks and adversaries would get them to pay rapt attention to what you tell them.

In the same vein, this message would have to change as you converse with the line managers, training managers or HR managers. With these leaders, it's more about the nitty-gritty, the specific details, and the cybersecurity program's ins and outs. Of course, security of income and profitability are also vital to them. Still, they also want to ensure that their employees don't spend too much time learning how to use your cybersecurity solution and would be very much interested in the ease of using your product without having to call on you now and then.

CHAPTER EIGHTEEN

CYBERSECURITY TECHNOLOGIES, SERVICE COMPONENTS AND BENEFITS

This chapter is dedicated to helping you understand various cybersecurity technologies, solutions and components that clients need. Ultimately, by understanding what and where all of the "cybersecurity technologies" pieces fit, you will be armed with valuable insight to help understand your client's business needs and requirements. We have taken information from industry accepted definitions. [12]

More importantly, depending on what security products and services you sell, it is critical to know how they fit relative to other security solutions. This is important as CISOs and CIOs have their priority lists. CISOs and their teams must leverage many security solutions to keep their organizations compliant, secure and productive. There is no single technology or solution that solves every possible security issue. CISOs and their teams must take a risk-based approach and carefully determine how to allocate resources to security tools and solutions (i.e. funding, staffing, etc.).

Below we list and define each Cybersecurity Technology and solution segment that many CISOs and their teams employ. Please note that

12   Gartner. n.d. "Information Technology (IT) Glossary - Essential Information Technology (IT) Terms & Definitions." Gartner. Accessed April 11, 2022. https://www.gartner.com/en/information-technology/glossary.

we are only scratching the surface, and as such, the list and definitions below are non-exhaustive and high-level.

ENDPOINT PROTECTION PLATFORMS (EPP)

EPP solutions aim to secure end-user devices from various threats, such as malware and ransomware. EPP solutions typically use agents that reside on endpoint devices. These include desktops, mobiles, laptops, and other devices that interface with the corporate network (including hybrid multi-cloud environments). EPP can also include variants of bring-your-own-device (BYOD), which are user-owned devices with limited access to corporate data/resources (i.e. using a personal iPad to access the corporate Office 365 account).

EPP solutions evolved over the past several decades from traditional antivirus software. Today, EPP solutions provide more comprehensive protection to include features and functions such as:

- Anti-malware and endpoint policy controls; enforced by endpoint-based agents

- Holistic endpoint management tools

- Offering command and control capabilities of all managed endpoints

- Application control; (i.e. allow and block lists of approved applications).

- Endpoint detection and response (EDR); provides clients with comprehensive capabilities to handle various endpoint-centric threats/issues/anomalies.

- Threat hunting and Extended detection and Response (XDR) capabilities

- Vulnerability and patch management.

EPP solutions are vital to most modern-day organizations. Their teams might leverage EPP solutions with popular vendors offering EPP solutions, such as Microsoft, CrowdStrike, Sentinel One, and Trend Micro.

Since these solutions typically require agents deployed at the endpoint, migrating from one solution to another is no trivial effort.

Security leaders tend to have exhaustive and comprehensive sales cycles to determine the best fit.

DIGITAL IDENTITY - IDENTITY AND ACCESS MANAGEMENT (IAM)

In the physical world, we typically carry credentials, such as a Passport, driver's license, and other ID cards. A variety of identity providers issue these physical credentials; in the case of a Passport, the identity provider is the "issuing country". The identity provider validates your identity and ensures that you are bound to that credential (i.e. your picture, identity attributes such as a name, birthplace, etc.), thereby creating a trustworthy document. With a physical Passport in hand, you are now free to traverse the world with valid proof of your identity.

But what about in the digital world? Today, we do not have trustworthy "Passports" issued by identity providers that are globally accessible. Work is underway, but the market has a long way to go. When it comes to enterprise security and enterprise identity, organizations have long-held practices and technologies that allow them to identify new and existing employees and manage their ongoing access. And while these aren't perfect, these IAM tools and practices are widely used today.

There isn't much use of the term 'digital identity.' Rather, most security leaders leverage the time "identity and access management" or IAM.

Identity and access management (IAM) spans people, processes and technology. This section focuses on the core technologies that make up IAM.

According to Gartner,

Identity and access management (IAM) is the discipline that enables the right individuals to access the right resources at the right times for the right reasons.

However, the aforementioned definition is human-centric; in today's environment, IAM also needs to account for machines. Machines such as software bots, applications, and other non-human entities. All of these require identities and access rights and entitlements.

Security leaders do not just use IAM solutions but, in many cases, also human resources (HR) professionals, marketing, and/or digital experience teams. HR professionals leverage IAM tools when dealing with employees changing roles. Typically, the workflow will involve IT, HR, and a dedicated IAM team that overlaps with the security team. When dealing with consumer digital channels, marketing and digital experience professionals might also get involved with IAM. For example, a banking institution might include marketing and digital experience officers when reviewing the consumer experience of how customers might sign-up and sign in to their banking accounts. Indeed, security and compliance are critical here, but so is the consumer experience.

IAM isn't just limited to the security world; it can involve many other personas across the organization. Most organizations have user categories such as,

- **JOINERS**: These are new employees to the organization. They must be validated, and then given a role and entitlement assignment (i.e. for a user destined to be in the finance department; they should have access to finance systems such as payroll).

- **MOVERS**: Employees changing jobs or roles. Access entitlements might need to vary depending on their role. For example, if the user changes from finance to marketing, they likely do not need access to company payroll systems anymore. They might now need access to marketing automation software)

- **LEAVERS**: Employees that are leaving the organization. Their identities/access need to be terminated.

With all of that in mind, what are the critical subsets of IAM, and their definitions?

CRITICAL IAM SOLUTION AND TECHNOLOGY SUBSEGMENTS - A NON-EXHAUSTIVE LIST:

- **USER AUTHENTICATION**: Leverages various tools and solutions that introduce additional form factors to bolster the security of user authentication. Due to the market's current status, which is reliant on usernames and passwords, the market has been focused primarily on adding 'factors' to the authentication process. Otherwise known as Multi-factor authentication, or MFA, a user authenticates with their username and password and leverages a second factor, such as a one-time code, a biometric, or a USB token. More recently, this segment has been focused on "passwordless" authentication, whereby the use of the password is completely phased out. Passwordless authentication generally requires one or more secure devices that offer multiple authentication methods (i.e. biometrics) with the aim of strongly authenticating the user.

SAMPLE VENDORS :1Kosmos, HYPR, Transmit Security, and Trusona.

- **ACCESS MANAGEMENT (AM)**: Access management, simply means managing the access and entitlements of employees, partners, and customers. Historically, these solutions were primarily on-premise; and there were several legacy categories.

However, today, AM solutions are especially cloud-based. They offer several capabilities:

- **SINGLE SIGN-ON (SSO)**: Sign in once, and the service via federation protocols and secure mechanisms facilitates SSO across several applications. For example, a user strongly authenticates into an access portal. They would see several applications (icons) from that portal that they could simply click on; the AM service facilitates the secure "SSO" into the requested application. AM solutions offer additional IAM capabilities, such as MFA/Passwordless authentication, Bring Your Own Identity (BYOI) social login support, and user self-service portals.

SAMPLE VENDORS: ForgeRock, IBM, Okta, Bloksec, and Ping Identity.

- **PRIVILEGED ACCOUNT MANAGEMENT (PAM)**: These tools focus on managing and protecting privileged user accounts privileged users can vary, but typically, they are power users or administrators with critical entitlements within the organization. These users are viewed as "privileged" because they likely have access to critical corporate systems and data. Attackers aim to compromise these users due to their valuable access entitlements. PAM tools aim to help organizations govern, monitor, and control these sensitive accounts. PAM tools today are critical, and as such, many auditors and advisors highly recommend that these tools be in place.

SAMPLE VENDORS: BeyondTrust, and CyberArk.

- **MACHINE IDENTITY MANAGEMENT:** While the management of humans is critical, so is the creation and management of machine identities. Machines, in this case, are software, websites, IoT devices, applications, and/ or bots (i.e. a chatbot). These entities may or may not be supervised by a human, but they need digital identities to be authenticated and authorized to access corporate systems and data. While this is a newer field, expect this area to expand over the coming years, especially as "automation" takes hold, whereby organizations leverage bots to automate mundane and tedious tasks (i.e. fielding chats with customers, parsing through data to identify trends, etc).

Bots might have similar behaviour patterns to humans. Still, they could also vary dramatically (i.e. a bot can complete business work in the blink of an eye compared to a human). This area will undoubtedly introduce new solutions, models and approaches to security.

SAMPLE VENDORS: AppViewX, KeyFactor, Sectigo and Venafi.

MOBILE SECURITY - ENTERPRISE MOBILITY MANAGEMENT (EMM)

EMM, also known as Mobile device management (MDM), has evolved over the past decade to include many variants of mobile devices and endpoints. This is because mobile devices such as phones and tablets differ from traditional endpoints like Windows and macOS laptops. Whether BYOD or corporate-issued and owned, mobile devices, much like endpoints, require security. While some EPP solutions and vendors offer some mobile functionality, most complex organizations leverage some kind of EMM. From a high level, security leaders typically secure mobile environments with EMM solutions as they empower security leaders to manage the mobile device fleet from an OS and application control perspective. Depending on the OS level support, EMM solutions can control by way of policy elements such as

- Vulnerability and Patch Management

- Prevention of malware, and jailbroken devices

- Manage Carrier connectivity (i.e. set data limits)

- Enable VPN, Remote access

- BYOD Management and control

- Application Management

  SAMPLE VENDORS IN THE EMM SPACE: BlackBerry, IBM, Ivanti and VMWare

- **DATA SECURITY:** Today every business relies on data to build new products, respond to customer demands, and to compete. Data-driven businesses such as Amazon, Google, Meta (formerly Facebook) and Uber are precious companies because their data amplifies and/or acts as the basis for their offerings. Data is now the new oil. Whether it is consumer activity information, credit card numbers, health data, or intellectual property, security leaders know that their organizations store and use a lot of valuable data. Unfortunately, attackers also know this as well. This data shows that bad actors seek to steal and/or lock up with ransomware. Data security tools are no longer an option for security leaders and their organizations. Below is a non-exhaustive list of popular data security solutions and tools:

- **DATA CLASSIFICATION:** These tools allow organizations to classify or label data, such as files, documents, and emails. Various enterprise security tools that scan content would leverage data classification as a contextual element for policy enforcement. For example, a user could label a Microsoft Word document as "classified" to denote that the document is sensitive and likely should only be viewed/sent to other users that are authorized. If the user accidentally sends the document to an unauthorized user via email, the email filter would block the document, triggered by the data's classification of "sensitive" based on a corporate policy. Data loss prevention solutions and email security solutions benefit significantly from data classification tools, as it allows them to understand further sensitivity levels of data (we cover these tools below).

There are two approaches to data classification from a high level: user-driven and automated. Like the example above, (user-driven) is when a user sets the classification of a document/data (typically via a drop-down box, within the applications, such as Microsoft Word). Automated classification is generally when the data/file is sent through an email or DLP agent; these agents could scan the file/data, and if there is a pattern match to a sensitive data type (i.e. a credit card number format, social security/insurance number, etc.), the file could be automatically classified in line with the corporate policy. While there are stand-alone data classification tools, the ongoing trend is that data classification functionality is being offered by various other solution offerings, such as other data security products, built in natively to office productivity suites, and/or cloud platforms. However, classification alone is not enough; security leaders must leverage other tools to use data classification as a contextual input.

SAMPLE VENDORS: Helpnet Systems (Titus), IBM, Varonis and Microsoft.

- **DATA LOSS PREVENTION (DLP)**: DLP tools leverage data classification and labels/tags, to help security leaders enforce policies when it comes to content control and inspection. Ultimately, DLP solutions aim to prevent data leakage, either initiated by bad actors or by accident (i.e. a user accidentally sending a sensitive document outside the company). DLP functions can focus and span areas in the corporate network such as web, email and endpoints. That is providing DLP and content security across these vectors.

SAMPLE VENDORS: Cisco, Digital Guardian, Forcepoint, Microsoft, Netscope, and Proofpoint

- **ENCRYPTION AND CRYPTOGRAPHY:** Encryption is one of the tried and tested ways to ensure that data is stored in a protected state. Although savvy and motivated attackers can find ways around it, it is typically seen as the best defence when protecting corporate data.

Nevertheless, in almost every environment you encounter, your prospects and clients have multiple levels of encryption, powered by numerous cryptography products and services. And while we could easily write a whole chapter on cryptography, we aim to give you a high-level view of the subject.

- **DATA PROTECTION IN MOTION:** Otherwise known as Transport Layer Security (TLS); this is the backbone of all internet and digital communications today (well, almost all!). The most widespread use of this technology is with websites and networks today. SSL/TLS digital certificates are used to identify websites and/or the networks you aim to access. For the case of the web, when your browser encounters a website, say "amazon.com" - it establishes an "https" session triggered by Amazon's digital certificate. Your browser seamlessly authenticates Amazon's certificate and initiates a TLS session. This is an encrypted tunnel between your browser and Amazon's website.

Similarly, this flow is replicated when you access a corporate network (say remotely, via a virtual private network or VPN). The main technology leverage here today is Public-Key Infrastructure (PKI).

SAMPLE VENDORS: DigiCert, Let's Encrypt and Sectigo

- **DATA PROTECTION AT REST:** As the name implies, this is for data residing in data repositories such as databases, cloud storage, or on hard drives. Files, folders or entire hard drives could be encrypted to prevent unauthorized access. The user requires a cryptographic key to encrypt, which "unlocks" the data. This cryptographic key is usually tied to the user's digital identity; good best practices would have the user strongly authenticate to initiate usage of the cryptographic key to unencrypt the data. As mentioned above, most organizations today typically leverage one or more encryption tools. These tools are generally called

Encryption Key Management; Sample vendors. Thales, Townsend Security and Virtru.

- **PUBLIC-KEY INFRASTRUCTURE (PKI)**: PKI is the foundation for digital trust, and good best practices would have any digital interactions leverage PKI. From modern-day passports, identity cards, and blockchain systems, to passwordless authentication, all leverage PKI as the digital trust foundation. However, because PKI is a foundational technology, it is not a direct solution. But rather, it enables security within many use cases and applications. Use case areas such as:

- Passwordless Authentication

- Digital Signatures

  - » Digital Document Signing

- Code Signing (to ensure integrity and validity of code)

- Email Encryption via a protocol S/MIME

- Mobile Device and IoT Identity & security

  - » PKI is suited well to provide device identity

- Website identity and authentication

- Robotic Process Automation (RPA) security

  SAMPLE VENDORS: DigiCert, Entrust, and Sectigo

- **EMAIL SECURITY**: Many critical business communications occur via email. As such, secure email is paramount for business. Unfortunately, attackers know that most consumers and employees leverage email for critical use. As such, email is a popular method for attackers to leverage. Whether it be with phishing attacks, spam, and/or emails with malicious links, the aim is to direct you to a website/ location whereby your system seamlessly downloads malware. Therefore, email-based attacks have caused many security leaders to invest in tools and technology to help. Some of the core functionality of email security spans:

- Anti-Spam / Phishing / Malware

  » The Email security tool aims to block such malicious emails and attachments

- DLP

  » As discussed above, some email tools come with DLP capabilities; to prevent data loss.

- Email Encryption

  » As mentioned above in the PKI section, the most popular email clients today support S/MIME, enabling encrypted emails. In addition, users can also 'digitally sign' their emails to mitigate tampering/modification in transit.

  SAMPLE VENDORS: Barracuda, Cisco, Mimecast, Proofpoint, and Trend Micro

- **WEB SECURITY:** Websites are mission-critical for every business today. Whether accessing web-based systems or content, organizations depend on the web for business. But the web isn't safe; even trustworthy sites could become compromised and host malware. In addition, inappropriate content could be accessed on corporate systems, exposing the organization to security and reputational/brand-damaging risks. As such, web security and filtering tools aim to provide security leaders with the ability to control and block websites and protect users from malicious payloads, such as malware. Finally, today's attacks leverage a one-two punch, where the attacker sends an email with an embedded link. The attack's goal is to have the user visit the compromised website, where malware could be seamlessly downloaded. It is mission critical for security leaders to employ both email and web security tools.

  SAMPLE VENDORS: Cisco and Forcepoint.

- **APPLICATION SECURITY:** Many organizations today have developers that build various internal/external applications. These could be mobile apps, web apps, or other cloud-based applications. Issues at the code level could unfortunately expose organizations to security issues. As such, application security tools aim to provide developers with solutions to find potential security issues with code and/or practices. This includes the fast-growing area of developer operations or DevOps. Attackers often scan applications and code, looking to find vulnerabilities to exploit. Many organizations have application and DevOps security tools to help secure the application development process.

SAMPLE VENDORS: Micro Focus, Veracode, Synopsys.

- **NETWORK SECURITY**: From firewalls, to wireless security, to virtual private networks (VPNs), network security is common for all organizations. And while much of this is changing with the advent of hybrid and multi-cloud environments, most organizations still have a significant on-premise environment. Common network security tools and components are:

- Firewalls:

  » Control all inbound/outbound network traffic. Firewalls aim to block malicious network traffic and prevent unauthorized intrusions. These tools focus on the network layer rather than protecting applications and data.

- Next-Generation Firewalls (NGFW)

  » An enhanced version of the standard category above, NGFWs focus on network level protections and provide malware and application-level security.

- Remote Access Virtual Private Network (VPN)

  » VPNs are common in most corporate environments. VPNs enable remote access to a corporate network. Many organizations employ VPN, typically later in additional identity-based security, to ensure that only authorized users and devices may connect to the VPN. This is generally done by pairing VPN with MFA/Passwordless authentication.

SAMPLE VENDORS: Checkpoint, Cisco, Fortinet and Palo Alto Networks

CLOUD SECURITY: Today, many organizations have significant investments in cloud-based systems. As a result, many have migrated to the cloud, but with demands for security. Cloud security spans a wide array of segments, such as:

CLOUD ACCESS SECURITY BROKERS (CASBS): CASBs aim to provide security leaders with visibility and control of their cloud-based environments. A CASB typically sits between the organization and the various multi-cloud environments, where the CASB can monitor, enforce and report on cloud activities. Security leaders can ensure a consistent security policy and enforcement across the multi-cloud with many disparate cloud environments.

SAMPLE VENDORS: Cisco, Microsoft, Netscope and Zscaler.

CLOUD POSTURE MANAGEMENT (CPSM): IT leaders can quickly and rapidly stand up cloud-based environments as they respond to business demands (i.e. standing up a new server for data storage). Creating a cloud-based environment can occur quickly, but it can be challenging to ensure that they are appropriately configured. Misconfigurations can lead to security and access vulnerabilities, exposing sensitive corporate information or worse. The CPSM cloud-security segment aims to help security and IT leaders deploy, maintain and manage secure cloud environments. These tools can conduct periodic assessments to manage and solve any potential critical misconfigurations.

SAMPLE VENDORS: Orca Security, Trend Micro, and Zscaler.

CLOUD WORKLOAD PROTECTION (CWP): One major benefit of cloud-based services is that some offer elastic virtual services to serve clients' various on-demand computing needs. Otherwise known as cloud workloads, they can be applications or services that run cloud-based virtual machines, databases, or containers. These environments are similar to on-prem but differ in how they are configured and managed. CWP tools offer protection specific for these cloud-based workloads and are becoming much more common in modern-day cloud-focused environments.

SAMPLE VENDORS: Orca Security, Trend Micro, and Zscaler.

CYBERSECURITY AND BUZZ WORDS: WHAT IS THE DEAL WITH ZERO TRUST, AND IDENTITY-FIRST SECURITY?

For the past several years, the Cybersecurity market has increased in market value. According to Fortune Business Insights, the cybersecurity market is expected to reach $366 billion US by 2028.[13] With all this growth, vendors large, small, and emerging, are all gearing up to take a piece of the pie. Yet, with the flurry of activity, many try to differentiate themselves by "creating a new category", or "disrupting others" in their respective cybersecurity market segment.

One outcome of this growth and activity is the rampant use of buzzwords. Not all of them are bad; many are based on essential security fundamentals. As an aspiring cybersecurity professional, you will be exposed to these buzzwords; but what should you do? First of all, you should have a high-level understanding of the common buzzwords. They can change on a quarterly or yearly basis. Good old Google can be your best friend, but you will benefit from getting their opinions if you have industry contacts (such as industry analysts and CISOs). Asking them questions, such as:

- What Does BUZZWORD mean to you?

- Has the BUZZWORD trend impacted you?

- Do you see BUZZWORD changing how you do your job?

Fill in "BUZZWORD" with any major buzzwords, such as the ones listed here; i.e. Zero Trust, and Identity-First Security.

....

13 Fortune Business Insights™ Pvt. Ltd. 2022. "Cyber Security Market to Reach USD 366.10 Billion by 2028; Surging Number of E-Commerce Platforms to Amplify Market Growth: Says Fortune Business Insights." GlobeNewswire. https://www.globenewswire.com/news-release/2022/01/05/2361317/0/en/Cyber-Security-Market-to-Reach-USD-366-10-Billion-by-2028-Surging-Number-of-E-Commerce-Platforms-to-Amplify-Market-Growth-Says-Fortune-Business-Insights.html.

Point is, you need to be agile and always ready to read, watch and understand the implications of these buzzwords. Some might directly impact your specific segment today; others might signal a looming change.

As of the writing of this book, there is a wide range of terms that we could dissect and discuss, but we will focus on two buzz-words.

ZERO TRUST: Coined by Forrester, 'Zero Trust' is a popular term in cybersecurity. But beyond the hype and buzz, the National Institute of Standards and Technology (NIST), a widely respected standard and guidance body, recommends that organizations leverage "Zero Trust Architecture".[14] Ultimately, zero trust focuses on the fact that anyone at any time could attempt to access your corporate network, devices, and/or cloud resources. Some might be legitimate entities; others might be malicious; shifting the good and the bad is much more complex in today's digital environment. Many security leaders are looking to a zero-trust model to continuously verify and determine if the entity (devices, humans, or machines) is authenticated and trusted. While all of that is good in theory, security leaders tend to look for solutions that can solve "zero trust." But, in this case, there is no single solution. Zero trust is a mindset and approach and requires various tools, solutions, and processes. This is where some of the confusion lies in the market today, with some vendors pushing aggressive marketing terminology that gives security leaders the false impression that zero trust solves everything. Zero trust is a concept you should become familiar with, but be cautious of client and vendor claims.

IDENTITY-FIRST SECURITY: Introduced by Gartner in 2021, identity-first security emphasizes that all security must start with identity.[15] In other words, "identity is the new perimeter". For example, before you allow a new mobile device, or laptop to connect to your corporate network, you should first identify the device, then leverage good IAM practices to establish and maintain trust. Any and all of the security technologies we highlighted above should be connected back to some kind of identity. How can you conduct trustworthy business if you don't know who or what you are dealing with? While a relatively new term in the space, you should expect that you might get asked about

---

14   Borchert, Oliver, Scott Rose, Stu Mitchell, and Sean Connelly. 2020. "SP 800-207, Zero Trust Architecture | CSRC." NIST Computer Security Resource Center. https://csrc.nist.gov/publications/detail/sp/800-207/final.

15   Crandall, Carolyn. 2021. "Identity-first security redefined." ITProPortal. https://www.itproportal.com/features/identity-first-security-redefined/.

your solutions approach to "identity-first security". As such, what is your solution's identity angle? Does your solution integrate with IAM solutions and tools? Perhaps some that we listed above.

While these are just two examples, going forward, as a cybersecurity sales professional, you should brace for and expect more "buzzy" terms in the space of cybersecurity. It is important to understand what they are and how they might impact your specific job and/or solution. Who knows, a prospect might ask you - how does your security solution work with our "zero trust" project?

CYBERSECURITY MESH ARCHITECTURE (CSMA):

In 2021, and again in 2022, Gartner defined and highlighted the Cybersecurity mesh architecture (CSMA).

While we won't fully break down every element of CSMA, it is important to know what it is and why it is important.

What is CSMA? Cybersecurity mesh architecture is a concept, not a specific technology per se, that aims to unify, simplify and orchestrate enterprise cybersecurity technologies. Currently, most security teams struggle with too many security products that are siloed, and worse yet, vendors with proprietary and closed technologies that force lock-in. The unfortunate consequences of this are:

- Too many security products to manage and maintain

- Increased cybersecurity product complexity, which reduces and negatively impacts security analyst effectiveness when maintaining or responding to security incidents

  » Complicates threat hunting, due to analysts having to traverse multiple consoles

- The introduction of Hybrid-Multi-Cloud Environments further complicating visibility, management and orchestration

CSMA aims to change that. Some of the core aspects of CSMA are (non-exhaustive list):

- Leverage security products and services that are interoperabile and open (i.e. offer open APIs for customization)

> » **OPENNESS:** CSMA recommends that products and services use open standards, such that various and ancillary security products can push/pull information.

> » **INTEROPERABILITY:** CSMA encourages that products and services leverage integrations with common enterprise products and services.

SCALABLE: With openness and interoperability in mind, they must also be scalable to support further business growth.

COMPOSTABLE AND MODULAR MESH ARCHITECTURE: CSMA highlights "layers" which, by way of open and interoperable standards, could be expanded and extended to allow for future-proofing and/or use case or threat realization.

As time goes on, CISOs and their teams that successfully leverage concepts of CSMA will be able to respond to incidents more effectively, reducing cognitive load on security analysts. In addition, they will position themselves for financial success by saving money, through consolidating expensive and low value security products and services. Ultimately, CISOs and their teams will be better armed to securely enable desirable business outcomes, versus simply being a barrier to the business.

Already, some security platform vendors have committed to providing clients with CSMA frameworks. Vendors such as: Fortinet, F5, and VMWare.

CYBERSECURITY AWARENESS & TRAINING FOR ENTERPRISES

Organizations face threats from complex criminal organizations and nation-state hackers, and your client's organization is not different. To mitigate the risks posed by these cybercriminals, they must protect their organization's proprietary and sensitive information. Also, they must commit to training their employees to do all they can to protect proprietary and sensitive information. Cybersecurity awareness and training programs help your client educate their employees on cybersecurity threats, risks, and best practices, including how they can respond to the ever-changing and evolving threat landscape.

Cybersecurity includes personnel, policies, and technology. In addition, the threat landscape is constantly changing, and threats take advantage of human error or negligence and system vulnerabilities. Therefore, your client must ensure that their workers are aware of these vulnerabilities and provide adequate training to keep them abreast of the constantly evolving threat landscape.

Due to the recent shift to remote work, organizations now understand that cybersecurity needs to be part of the organizational culture. Cybersecurity is essential whether your client's employees work from home or in an office environment. In addition, your client must understand the importance of employee training programs to the organization and the need for them to put in place adequate security policies and controls.

Recently, TalentLMS21 conducted a survey of 1,200 US employees to assess their awareness and knowledge of cybersecurity risks. TalentLMS also tested employees on basic cybersecurity principles.

The survey results showed that only 69% of respondents received cybersecurity training from their current employers. Given the recent worldwide events and cyberattacks involving almost every department, every organization with information technology employees should require its employees to participate in annual cybersecurity awareness and training. Failure to provide employees with cybersecurity training increases the risk of violations related to human error.

In addition, cybersecurity awareness and training are only part of the success equation. You must also ensure that your clients focus their energy and resources on building a culture of cybersecurity by hiring people with the right attitude towards cybersecurity.

Additionally, they must conduct regular awareness training and testing for their employees and provide them with rewards and recognitions to reinforce the desired behaviours.

BENEFITS OF CYBERSECURITY AWARENESS AND TRAINING FOR ENTERPRISES

What are the reasons that justify cybersecurity awareness and training for workers in my client's organization? You might ask. The reasons are not entirely far-fetched. One of the significant reasons for cybersecurity awareness and training is realizing that cybercrimes have been around for a long time and are not leaving. Instead, they are getting more brazen.

As the connectivity and advancement of technology continue to rise, the methods of perpetrating cyber attacks continue to evolve.

Being very much aware that your client relies on the continued integrity of their network, you must see, in this situation, a reason to ensure they entrench adequate cybersecurity that guarantees the safety of their network.

Other reasons (or benefits) of cybersecurity awareness and training include the following:

BETTER INFORMATION SECURITY

Having organization-tailored cybersecurity controls and policies is a crucial part of your client's organization's operation. Cybersecurity awareness training programs will help bring the staff members of your client's organization up-to-date with the organization's security procedures, policies, and best practices. Aside from assisting the workers to stay aware of these cybersecurity policies, the training also helps them follow and understand the procedures.

HELPS PREVENT CYBER-RELATED INCIDENTS

Suppose your client wants to create a culture of cybersecurity in their workplace. In that case, training employees about safe online computing, strong passwords, social engineering, and more are essential in turning their organization into the first line of cyber defence while also ensuring that sensitive business data remain confidential.

HELPS TO KEEP CLIENTS AND SHAREHOLDERS SATISFIED

A data breach can permanently damage any customers' confidence in your client's organization. It can even cause some clients to leave, while some might pursue legal recourse leading to even more damage. However, by investing in innovative and comprehensive cybersecurity training to educate their staff members, customers can be at ease knowing that their data is being handled by people that understand security risks.

Additionally, suppose it is evident to investors that you provide adequate training for your staff members. In that case, they become more aware of the value of cybersecurity controls and have more trust in your client's organization.

HELPS TO SAVE MONEY

The damages that come with cyber-related incidents can be expensive and detrimental to your client's organization's reputation. Therefore, the benefit they get from investing in security awareness training far outweighs the cost of a leak or breach. The following are some potential issues that might come with a cyber-attack on your client's organization's network:

- Revenue loss

- Loss of organizational integrity

- Loss of clients

- Disruption of organizational operation

- Lawsuits

- Intellectual property (IP) theft

- Personally identifiable information (PII) theft

- Compromise and loss of client data and sensitive business information

Therefore, by ensuring that your client has a well-established and active program to train staff members about cybersecurity, they are keeping their organization safe from the above problems while also providing the sustained integrity of their network.

BOLSTERS EMPLOYEE CONFIDENCE

Keeping employees updated with the latest cyber threat intelligence and attack methods will help them stay confident regardless of the constant cybersecurity uncertainty. Cybersecurity training also enables your client to eliminate risky behaviour and instill security company-wide best practices across their organization.

By making cybersecurity a priority for their company, your client's employees will have access to the advanced tools and resources they need for adequate training. That, in turn, enables staff to share among themselves for safe technology usage. There are various cybersecurity training options for your client and their organization. Whichever you choose, the result is the promotion of awareness.

Our next topic is,

INFORMATION SECURITY SERVICE

Information security is a set of practices designed to protect personal data from unauthorized access and modification during storage or transmission from one place to another.

Information security is designed and implemented to protect print, electronic, and other private, sensitive, and personal data from unauthorized persons. In addition, it is used to protect data from being misused, leaked, modified, and destroyed.

Information security and network security are often used interchangeably, but they are not the same. Network security is a practice used to provide online attack security, and information security is a specific network security discipline.

There are some essential components of information security which are discussed below.

Confidentiality is one of the critical elements in information security. The data is confidential when only authorized persons can access the data. To ensure confidentiality, your client will be required to use techniques that beef up network security, such as strong passwords, encryptions, and other security measures that defend against potential attacks.

Network Integrity implies the maintenance of data and preventing the same from being accidentally or maliciously tampered with. Techniques used for confidentiality can protect data integrity because cybercriminals cannot change data when they cannot access it.

Usability is another fundamental element of information security. Your clients need to ensure that unauthorized persons do not access their data and that only those with permission can access it. The availability of information security means matching network and computing resources to calculate data access and implement better strategies for disaster recovery purposes.

INFORMATION SECURITY POLICY

An information security policy is a document that your client may create. Its purpose is to communicate the organization's intent, objectives and goals for information security and form the foundation of its information security program. It helps determine the data that needs to be protected and how to protect it. These policies guide your client's organization in the decision-making process regarding the choice of cybersecurity tools. It also states the behaviour and responsibilities of their employees.

Some of the topics your client's organization's information security policy should include are;

i. *The purpose of the information security program and objectives*

ii. *The key terms are used in the document to ensure that everyone understands them*

iii. *Organization's password policy*

iv. *Staff members with access to specific data*

v. *The role of employees in safeguarding organization and client data*

BENEFITS OF INFORMATION SECURITY SERVICES

Some of the justifications for information security include the following:

SECURE THE REPUTATION FOR DOING BUSINESS

Data breaches damage your client's reputation, undermine the trust between your client and their customers, and send a message that your client's organization is not trustworthy and that they do not take appropriate steps to protect customers' privacy and security. However, if you help your clients prioritize data protection and information security, they will be able to maintain their organizations' reputations.

STRENGTHENS DATA PROTECTION SKILLS

Maintaining a strategy with data protection requirements starts with tracking which confidential information customers access and seamlessly changing your organization's information.

For example, companies subject to the European GDPR must support their customers' right to access the data they collect. GDPR allows organizations to store all sensitive information about users and how they use such data and where it is stored, as required by customers. That means customers need to know where the data is stored and access the information promptly.

According to the GDPR, companies must collect data from users who opt-in to the data collection process and "forget" users when requested, delete all their data, and stop disseminating such data.

These standards have prompted IT departments to update their data processing systems to respect the privacy of customers and improve operational performance. First, you need to ensure that your client reviews their current data systems to ensure that customers have opted into their data collection plans. After the audit, they will have to delete the customer's non-opt-in data files and introduce an organizational structure to index and scan data. After that, many tools can be used to classify data further, add additional value, and identify new marketing opportunities.

STRENGTHEN BUSINESS CULTURE

You can help your client build an internal organizational culture and external brand image that shows your client's dedication to customer privacy and protection.

In an era when so many large multinational companies are forced to disclose data breaches to millions of customers, your client will gain employee loyalty and promote mutual pride by taking reasonable measures to protect consumer information. This pride in a strong security mission and culture can be translated into internal compliance that meets daily security requirements and stricter compliance with company policies supporting data security and limiting risk.

PROMOTE TRANSPARENCY AND ACCESS CONTROL

An effective IT security policy system for your client ensures that only people with appropriate credentials can access their sensitive customer data security systems and databases. If the client effectively implements security management systems, they must ensure that access to such systems is controlled at the organizational level. They must also ensure that system activity is recorded to be traced back to the source. This monitoring method is a crucial measure to avoid opportunistic data leakage. First, you must make sure that your clients keep a list of approved individuals who have access to data. Then, they will have to check the list regularly to indicate changes in employee positions and status. They must also incorporate the removal of security clearances into the exit procedures of all business personnel to ensure that no former employees can access the company network in a way that might lead to data leakage.

Putting all of these information security mechanisms in place can effectively protect the security of customer data and proprietary data owned by your client's organization.

NETWORK SECURITY SERVICE

Network security is any system, device, or operation designed to protect your network's security, reliability, and data. Network security manages access to your client's network by preventing various threats from entering and spreading through the network.

Network security protects Internet-connected systems and networks from initial attacks such as hackers or viruses. The focus of network security is to protect your client's files, documents, and information from attacks. Most commonly, network security first authenticates using a username and password. Still, it can also use other tools such as firewalls, antivirus programs, and virtual private networks (VPNs) to protect network information.

TYPES OF NETWORK SECURITY

There are various types of network security services. Each of the available kinds has its specific use cases and importance. However, they all work together to help your client achieve and maintain healthy network security and keep their network from malware, attacks, and data loss.

ANTIVIRUS AND ANTI-MALWARE SOFTWARE

Malware attack your network in many forms, including viruses, worms, Trojan horses, spyware, or ransomware. Some malicious software will cause immediate theft or destruction of data, while others are more covert and take some time before secretly infiltrating systems and information.

Top antivirus and anti-malware programs will scan and monitor malicious software when entering the network and continuously monitor suspicious behaviour and abnormal conditions on the network to help reduce risks and prevent threats.

WIRELESS SECURITY

Wireless security refers to any measures taken to prevent susceptibility from installing wireless systems such as wireless local area networks (or LANs) that are particularly vulnerable to attacks.

Developing a cybersecurity plan that suits your organization is not complicated. Tools such as visual network maps can help your client comprehensively respond to threats and prevent future threats. Research and preparation are the best way to prevent malicious attacks, and a comprehensive network security solution is the best way to protect an organization's network infrastructure.

ACCESS CONTROL

Your client's network can have as many visitors as possible. However, not all visitors should have the same level of access. Access control helps control access to sensitive areas within your client's network. It does this by identifying each user on the network. The client can restrict access to known users and devices and block or restrict access to unrecognized devices and users.

APPLICATION SECURITY

Cybersecurity is not only about the integrity of your client's systems. It is also about the integrity of the systems that support operations in the network. Therefore, the client must review every device, software product, and application in use in their network to prevent infiltration through third-party networks. Application security, therefore, is the practice of avoiding any vulnerabilities caused by the integration of third-party systems and applications.

Many companies are migrating their data storage facilities to the cloud to benefit from increased efficiency, lower costs, integrated tools, and easier collaboration, especially among remote employees. However, cloud migration also brings some challenges. For example, when users can directly connect to the Internet, your client might find it hard to understand what their employees are doing, leading to an increase in the risk of data leakage. Cloud computing security may include encryption and identity management to solve this problem.

DISTRIBUTED DENIAL OF SERVICE PREVENTION (DDOS)

DDoS attacks are an increasingly common threat that causes the system to crash through many attempts to connect to work. DDoS protection tools will carefully check the incoming traffic of illegal connection requests and direct the traffic away from your network firewall.

DATA LOSS PREVENTION (DLP)

Data loss prevention (DLP) technology prohibits employees and network users from sharing sensitive information with users outside the network, whether accidentally or maliciously. Data loss may include uploading, downloading, and forwarding private files, printing personal information, and sharing access codes to confidential data.

EMAIL SECURITY

Email security vulnerabilities are the most common threat to network security. Attackers can use personal information and sophisticated marketing and social engineering strategies to trick people into accepting phishing campaigns, downloading malware, and following suspicious links. Email security applications help your client block incoming attacks, filter potential threats and prevent outgoing emails from sharing specific data or spreading malware through their network's contact list.

INTRUSION PREVENTION SYSTEMS (IPS)

Intrusion prevention systems (or IPS) scan system traffic to stop threats proactively. They can do this by tracking the progress of suspicious files and malware, mining complex digital data, and ultimately preventing the spread of the outbreak and preventing the system from reinfecting.

NETWORK SEGMENTATION

Network segmentation is a very effective way of improving your organization's security. By dividing network traffic into different areas or data sets with similar compliance requirements, your client can streamline the work of their security team. That makes it easier for them to apply and enforce security policies, and limit access and authorization to specific users. It also offers protection in BYOD (bring-your-own-device) environments.

FIREWALL

The firewall acts as a boundary between a trusted internal system and an unverified external network. Firewalls help protect your client's network by monitoring incoming requests against a set of network rules and policies that they have previously established.

SECURITY INFORMATION AND EVENT MANAGEMENT (SIEMS)

SIEM technology is similar to an intrusion prevention system (IPS), providing real-time analysis of network traffic and historical data, and providing system administrators with a complete view of network activity. This information is then combined with an intrusion detection system to enable network security personnel to identify and respond to potential threats.

VIRTUAL PRIVATE NETWORK

A virtual private network (or VPN) provides network protection for remote work by encrypting the connection between the endpoint and the network or system (usually via the Internet).

In most cases, remote access VPNs use Internet Protocol Security (IPsec) or Secure Sockets Layer (SSL) to verify communication from the device to the secure network.

BENEFITS OF NETWORK SECURITY

Now that we know about network security and the different divisions that constitute it, let us examine why your clients should have a network security service in their organization.

Many benefits accrue to network security services. As more companies undergo digital transformation, digital infrastructure security has become the top priority of every operations manager.

A safe and reliable network does not just protect the interests and operations of your organization; it also covers the interests of customers who exchange information with your organization and the public. Below are some other valuable reasons (or benefits) for your client to invest in network security services for their organization.

ESTABLISH TRUST

The security of large systems translates into the safety of everyone in an organization. In addition, cybersecurity (particularly the security of your client's network) enhances customers' confidence in the organization and protects your client's business from security breaches, reputation loss, and legal impact.

REDUCE RISK

Choosing a good network security service will help your client's business comply with business and government regulations. In cases of violation of these regulations, network security services will help the client minimize the business and financial impact.

PROTECT PROPRIETARY INFORMATION

Your client's customers rely on the organization to protect their sensitive information. Likewise, the client's business depends on the same protection. Network security, therefore, ensures that the information and data shared across your client's organizational networks are kept secure.

ACHIEVE A MORE MODERN WORKPLACE

From allowing employees to use VPNs to work safely from any location to encouraging collaboration through secure network access; network security provides options for future work. It also offers many levels of security that allow your clients to scale their network security along with growing business.

CLOUD SECURITY

Cloud security is a form of network security. Cloud security services help your client protect the data stored online through their cloud computing platform from theft, leakage, and accidental or intentional deletion. The methods you can explore to provide your client with cloud security include firewalls, penetration testing, obfuscation, tokenization, virtual private networks (VPN), and avoiding public Internet connections.

Cloud security helps your client create multiple levels of control within their organization's network to provide continuity and protection for cloud-based assets like websites and web applications. Your clients have to balance DDoS protection, high availability, data security, and regulatory compliance among their cloud security providers, whether in public or private clouds.

Cloud security is a set of control-based security measures and technical protection designed to protect the resources your clients have stored online from leakage, theft, or cloud data loss. The protection offered by cloud security services covers the organization's cloud infrastructure, applications, and data from threats.

CATEGORIES OF CLOUD SECURITY SERVICES

There are various cloud security services available for your client's organization. Let us look at some of these available services and how they help you keep your organization's network safe and threat-free.

1. **IDENTITY AND ACCESS MANAGEMENT:** This category of cloud security services provides controls for assured identity and access management. Identity and access management includes the personnel, processes, and systems used to manage access to corporate resources by ensuring that the entity's identity is verified and the correct access level is granted based on the determined identity. The application/solution usually keeps a log of activities, such as successful and failed authentication and access attempts.

2. **DATA LOSS PREVENTION**: This helps your client monitor, protect and verify the security of static data, dynamic data, and data available for cloud and local use. Data loss prevention services usually provide data protection to your client's organization by running on a desktop/server as some client while creating rules around what can be done. Data loss prevention services can be provided as part of the build in the cloud so that all your client's servers have data loss prevention software installed and a set of agreed rules deployed.

3. **NETWORK SECURITY**: This offers real-time protection, which can be provided locally through software/device installation, a proxy through the cloud, or by redirecting network traffic to a cloud provider. Network security also provides an additional layer of protection on top of content such as AV to prevent malware from entering your network through activities like web browsing.

4. **EMAIL SECURITY**: This provides control over inbound and outbound emails. It helps your client protect the organization from phishing and malicious attachments. It also enforces corporate policies while also providing business continuity options. Email security services allow your clients to implement policy-based email encryption and integrate encryption across various email server products. Many cloud email security services allow for the identification and non-repudiation of digital signatures.

5. **INTRUSION MANAGEMENT**: Pattern recognition is used to detect abnormal statistical events and react to them. Intrusion management allows for real-time reconfiguration of system components to prevent/prevent intrusions. Intrusion detection, prevention, and response methods in physical environments are mature; however, the growth of virtualization and large-scale multi-tenancy creates new intrusion targets and raises many questions about implementing the same protection in cloud environments.

6. **THE SECURITY INFORMATION AND EVENT MANAGEMENT SERVICE:** This cloud security service accepts logs and event information. The client can then correlate and analyze the data collected to provide real-time reports and alerts for event/events that may require intervention. They can also choose to keep logs in a tamper-proof manner so that the information can be used as evidence in any investigation.

7. **ENCRYPTION CLOUD SECURITY SERVICES:** They usually consist of algorithms that are computationally difficult or impossible to crack, as well as processes and procedures that manage encryption and decryption, hashing, digital signatures, certificate generation and renewal, and critical exchange.

BENEFITS OF CLOUD SECURITY SERVICES

There are many benefits accruing cloud security. Let us look at some of the significant benefits below.

PROVIDES CLOUD DDOS PROTECTION

Distributed denial of service attacks is rising, especially on retail and gaming websites. In 2014, reports22 showed that the frequency of DDoS attacks on client websites increased by almost 29%. Amplification attacks are DDoS attacks that use vulnerable systems to send significant traffic to target websites or web application servers. Amplification attacks, in particular, rose from only one occurrence in 2013 to 64 in 2014.

DDoS attacks are designed to overwhelm your network server to no longer respond to legitimate user requests. If a DDoS attack is successful, your client's network will be unusable for several hours or even days. That can lead to a colossal loss of revenue, customer trust, and organizational integrity (which you want to help your clients prevent.)

HIGH AVAILABILITY

Web assets are always open, whether it is an application suite or a commercial website. Security solutions that provide continuous real-time support (including real-time monitoring) are becoming a business necessity. CDN has enhanced the delivery of website content and application functions globally.

Some cloud security services have built-in flexibility to defend against various DDoS attacks. DDoS attacks can flood servers with traffic from 1Gbps to more than 20Gbps, which will make most of the original and backup servers in traditional network infrastructure unusable. Therefore, investing in cloud security for their network helps your client ensure that their network's continued availability and accessibility are held high.

DATA SECURITY

Several major data breaches by well-known companies made 2014 known as the "year of data breaches." After that, IT professionals and executives wanted to do everything they could to prevent data breaches in their companies. As a result, investments in access control, intrusion prevention, identity management, and virus and malware protection saw a noticeable increase.

If your clients combine these investments with network security protocols that protect communications between users and company servers, they get verified cloud security. Some cloud security services have added security protocols to their network. This will help your client protect sensitive information and transactions. For example, Transport Layer Security (TLS)-the successor to Secure Sockets Layer (SSL)-protects information to prevent third parties from eavesdropping or tampering with messages.

THE CLOSE

*"One who often thinks and reflects,
develops his foresight and vision."*

Ali ibn Abi Talib

Though the chapters of this book have officially concluded, your real journey is officially beginning.

Whether you are new to the world of cybersecurity sales, or a seasoned sales veteran, this book will serve as a guide for you, and compliment your personal evolution. You have now traveled through every stage of the sales process and have invested your personal time into refining the potential of your talent and your craft.

What you must remember is that the greatest and most indispensable talent you can master is the art of being yourself. Take what you have acquired from this book and integrate it into the spirit of what makes you, you. You now know and understand in its entirety that every sale is the development of a successful relationship.

Be sure to establish, nurture and prioritize the relationship you have with yourself.

It is your light, and it is powerful.

GLOSSARY

A/B TESTING: This is a process of depicting two variables of the same website page to different sects of web visitors.

B2B: Business to business. A business interaction between companies.

B2C: Business to consumer. It is the process of selling products or solutions to consumers who are the end-users.

BDM: Business Development Managers. They plan and coordinate sales and marketing initiatives.

BDRS: Business Development Representatives. They are an inside sales rep responsible for generating prospects via social selling, cold calling, cold email, and networking.

BOUNCE RATE: This is a metric that estimates the number of visits a user makes to your web page without actions before leaving.

BUYER PERSONA: This is a fictional representation of your target client. A clear picture of who you intend to sell to will enable you to create an effective sales strategy.

CTO: Chief Technology Officer. They direct the technology and related policies and processes in an organization.

CFO: Chief Financial Officer. They are responsible for the management of the financial operations of an organization.

CISO: Chief Information Security Officer. They are responsible for establishing and maintaining the organization's vision, business strategy, and activities to secure digital assets and technologies.

CEO: Chief Executive Officer. They are the highest-ranking executives in an organization responsible for making major decisions, managing overall operations and resources and act as the intermediary between the board of directors and company operations. They are also the face of the company in public places.

CSO: Chief Security Officer. They are responsible and accountable for an organization's cybersecurity posture and oversee security policies, programs, and compliance with regulatory standards.

CTA: Call-To-Actions. This is a sales and marketing term that points to the next step a salesperson wants the prospect to take after pitching to them. It always follows a marketing content or presentation.

CDN: Content Delivery Network. This is a distributed group of servers that collaborate to optimize the quick delivery of internet content to users.

CHURN RATE: Also known as the attrition rate. It is the rate at which clients stop transacting with a business.

DDOS: Distributed Denial of Service. A form of cyberattack where the cybercriminals disrupt network traffic, business server, and business organization service by overwhelming them with illegal requests.

GDPR: A legal framework that establishes guidelines on how businesses should source and process the personal information of consumers/users residing in the European Union (EU).

HR: Human Resources. Responsible for recruiting, onboarding and training company employees, coupled with other responsibilities that affect team productivity.

IT: Information technology. The use of computers to generate and share data for business operational purposes.

IP: Intellectual properties. Includes designs, applications, symbols, images, and names businesses use in commerce and are protected by laws such as trademarks, copyrights and patents.

LANS: Local Area Networks. LAN is a computer network that links computers in a defined location such as a university campus, business environment, school or residence.

METRICS: These are quantitative assessments utilized to analyze, compare, and track performance.

OKRS: Objective and Key Results. A framework for establishing and tracking sales objectives and outcomes.

PII: Personally Identifiable Information. Any data that defines users or consumers and can be distinguished from one person to another.

REFRAME: Reframe is a strategy that enables you to control sales calls, shift your thinking pattern and employ a different reference structure.

SALES CYCLE: This is a series of actions salespeople take to close a new client.

UNIQUE SELLING POINT: It is the essence that makes your product or service stands out when compared to competitors'

BIOS

DAVID MAHDI

Former Gartner IAM summit chair, and research VP, identity, cryptography and cybersecurity leader, David is an industry recognized subject matter expert. David has helped large organizations tackle digital transformation projects that included digital identity, IoT security, and early stage blockchain efforts; guided organizations to build internal cryptography teams, such as the cryptography centre of excellence; and consulted through IPOs, raising capital, and M&A, among many other contributions. A top performing analyst, his depth and breadth of coverage made him one of the most demanded industry analysts for clients around the globe. As a market maker, David was instrumental in creating markets and definitions for areas such as: Decentralized identity, Bring Your own identity (BYOI), passwordless authentication, Machine Identity management, and privacy enhanced computation.

In his current role of chief strategy officer (CSO) and CISO advisor at Sectigo, David leads the company's overall strategy, direction, and M&A efforts to expand its leadership in the digital trust space. David holds several board advisory positions for non-profits, and established technology providers in the areas of digital and decentralized Identity, post-quantum cryptography, cybersecurity awareness, and blockchain/NFTs. Previously, he held engineering, cybersecurity product and advisory roles at companies such as SecureKey, Entrust, Sophos and General Dynamics.

DANIEL PINSKY

Daniel is a cybersecurity professional with over 20 years of experience serving a variety of industries and sectors across North America and Europe. In that time, he has served and led across all domains including governance, program development, and the implementation and certification of various control frameworks.

He currently leads the national cyber security program and serves as the CSO and head of security governance and compliance for a Fortune 200 company.

Daniel studied business and technology, and holds a Bachelor of Commerce degree from McGill University. He also holds multiple certifications, including Certified Chief Information Officer (CCISO), CISM, CISA and CISSP.

Outside of work, Daniel is a Dale Carnegie Leadership Graduate and volunteers as a graduate coach. He is passionate about leadership, communication and personal development and shares insights through writing, speaking and mentoring.

KUSH SHARMA

Kush Sharma is award-winning leader and seasoned executive with 21 years of private and public sector experience across six industries. An active member of the cyber community, Sharma was named Global Enterprise CIO of 2020 related to digital architecture innovation, supported 3B+ in M&A and led teams through cyber breach responses first-hand. He has a strong reputation as a trusted advisor known for innovation, partnerships, and service delivery. Sharma ability to formulate a cyber vision and strategy, build an organization and then lead a team to operationalize vision. He also has experience in partnering with the Business to deliver over 20 Digital Transformation initiatives. These ranged between 2-10 years and 20M-1B in investment. Sharma worked with and managed diverse teams both onshore and offshore spanning multiple countries within a follow-the-sun operating model.

Kush is the founder of a cybersecurity and digital risk firm providing executive advisory and consulting services. He is also the CIO at Aptitude 360. Prior to this, he was the inaugural CISO for the City of Toronto and the inaugural Security & Compliance executive for Saputo where he established the cybersecurity organizations from the ground-up. Kush also worked at Accenture and Deloitte with a combined portfolio of over 50 clients advising on cybersecurity and digital transformation. He holds several industry certifications, is a frequent industry speaker and contributed to developing the Cyber Accountability Model Policy published by the World Economic Forum G20 Smart City Alliance.

VICTORIA VUONG

She has spent 13+ years in marketing supporting sales organizations, developing marketing strategies, and executing on them to create demand and build pipeline for companies such as Microsoft, Zscaler, Palo Alto Networks, and Check Point Software Technologies. Most recently Victoria is leading Zscaler's strategic technology alliance partnerships as the Sr. Partner Marketing Manager. Her primary areas of responsibilities include helping Zscaler build, grow, and scale AWS and Microsoft co-marketing + Marketplace programs and experiences.

JOHN PINARD

John is a CIO and Cybersecurity executive with over 30 years of business and IT leadership experience gathered through a variety of roles. He has held a variety of executive level roles in organizations ranging from Canada's leading retirement home company, many different CPG organizations, an IT Research organization, a non-profit provincial government regulator as well as a not-for-profit charitable organization. He has implemented and managed many mid-range to high-end applications like Oracle, SAP and Salesforce. In addition to his various roles, John is also a Cybersecurity speaker for SiberX (a leading provider of blog all, customized Cybersecurity training discussion platform) and holds a position on their Advisory Board.

John began his career as a Programmer Analyst and has worked his way up through his various careers at companies like Coca-Cola Ltd. and Makita Power Tools as well as a consulting role with a premium IBM Business Partner.

ABBAS KUDRATI

A long-time cybersecurity practitioner and CISO, Abbas is Microsoft Asia's Lead Chief Cybersecurity Advisor for the Security Solutions Area. In addition to his work at Microsoft, he serves as an executive advisor to Deakin University, LaTrobe University, HITRUST ASIA, EC Council ASIA, and several security and technology start-ups. He supports the broader security community through his work with ISACA Chapters and student mentorship.

He is a best selling authore for books such as, "Threat Hunting in the Cloud", "Zero Trust Journey Across the Digital Estate", and "Digitization Risks in Post Pandemic World".

He is also a part-time Professor of Practice with LaTrobe University and a keynote speaker on Zero-Trust, Cybersecurity, Cloud Security, Governance, Risk, and Compliance.

HASHIM HUSSEIN

Hashim is a Cyber Security Sales person with 10 years of experience helping public/private sector customers in their security transformations journey leveraging Cloud Security, Zero Trust and Secure Service Edge.

DANIEL EHRENREICH

Daniel is a consultant and lecturer acting at Secure Communications and Control Experts, and periodically teaches in colleges and presents at industry conferences on integration of cyber defense with industrial control systems; Daniel has over 30 years' engineering experience with ICS and OT systems for: electricity, water, gas and power plants as part of his activities at Tadiran, Motorola, Siemens and Waterfall Security. He has been selected as Chairman for the ICS Cybersec.

ALI KHAN

Having been brought up in over three continents as part of his childhood, Ali Khan, CCISO, CISM, CISSP, CDPSE, CISA also known as #thecyberAli, is an executive cybersecurity and risk management professional. Ali is also the co-author of a cybersecurity career handbook, *Because You Can: Your Cybersecurity Career*. With an "out-of-the box" thinking approach, Ali serves the cybersecurity industry globally with his innovative approach to executing and delivering on cybersecurity initiatives. With strong attention to detail, Ali builds a high level of trust and strong relationships with his clients to effectively execute on the complex requirements cybersecurity initiatives carry. As a mentor and educator, Ali continues to work closely with educational institutions to develop the next generation of cybersecurity professionals and also provides mentorship, guidance and career coaching to upcoming and aspiring cyber professionals and startups. Ali also volunteers his time and efforts at not-for-profit organizations providing his subject matter expertise. Ali has an Executive Management Certificate in Leading Organizations in Disruptive Times from INSEAD School of Business, France, an Honors Bachelor of Arts, majoring in information technology management from York University, Canada and is a Certified Chief

Information Security Officer (CCISO), Certified Information Security Manager (CISM), Certified Information Systems Security Professional (CISSP), Certified Data Privacy Solutions Engineer (CDPSE) and Certified Information Systems Auditor (CISA). Ali also has NATO and Level II (Secret) Clearance from the Government of Canada.

Ali is married to his beautiful wife, Shumaila and is blessed with three angel daughters, Dina, Amna and Zaina who are his gifts of this life.

Ali loves cars and likes to participate in a number of sports ranging from cricket, soccer and basketball. For more details, visit his website at www.thecyberali.com and follow him on online on social media platforms using hashtag #thecyberAli.

GEORGE Y. AL-KOURA, CD

George Y. Al-Koura, CD, is one of Canada's leading information security professionals. A security professional who boasts a highly diverse experiential background, George entered the cyber field in 2016 after a successful decade-long career as a Signals Intelligence Specialist with the Canadian Armed Forces (CAF). Starting in cyber as a Network Security Analyst at a global Managed Security Service Provider (MSSP), he quickly advanced his place in the industry by applying over a decade of military security intelligence and operations experience into the stand-up, sales, management and execution of multiple managed network security service offerings.

Before becoming a Chief Information Security Officer to multiple medium scale organizations in both the Defence and Social Platform spaces, George worked as a Senior Security Intelligence Advisor to multiple C-Suite officials at organizations ranging from provincial governments, major financial services institutes, and energy firms. He became a leading Canadian Cyber Threat Intelligence professional in 2018 after successfully standing up and taking to market a Managed CTI Service offering for a multinational consultancy. In 2019, he was one of the first commercial contractors in Canada tasked with monitoring various social media platforms for domestic and foreign actor interference during a provincial election on behalf of the government.

In terms of thought leadership, George has also served on multiple high-level government boards including the Defence Industry Advisory Group (DIAG) and CADSI Cyber Council. Though he has moved on from the Defence sector, George still maintains a close relationship with the public sector via his active involvement with the CIO Association of Canada.

KETAN KAPADIA

Ketan is the CEO & Co-Founder of BlokSec and Managing Director of Ipseity Security. He is an entrepreneur who is passionate about identity and cybersecurity. He has international experience working with institutions in North America, Europe, Africa, Australia, and Asia helping them from strategy through execution on their identity and security programs.

Throughout his 19+ years of experience in advisory/consulting and software development services he has led numerous engagements in defining and executing strategies supporting organizational risk reduction that is aligned with their business requirements and digital transformation. He is a frequent speaker at security events and conferences in North America and Africa, and is regularly engaged with C-suite leaders across various organizations in presenting complex identity and cybersecurity concepts that are simplified to support effective business transformation and cyber resilience.

KAREN NEMANI

Karen Nemani (she/her) is Founder and vCISO of Cyber Sage Security working with clients to transform and optimize their cybersecurity programs. With over two decades of experience working across all aspects of cybersecurity in multiple industries, Karen supports individuals and organizations in bridging business and cybersecurity needs and goals and works to align them to achieve optimal business success. Karen specializes in developing cybersecurity strategies, resilient security infrastructures and programs capable of growing and effectively managing their cybersecurity and enterprise risk. An advocate for women and diversity in the workplace, she is the Women in CyberSecurity (WiCyS) Ontario Affiliate President working to build community, open doors and create pathways for Canadian women in cybersecurity. Through Karen's leadership, WiCyS Ontario Affiliate was awarded the WiCyS 2022 International Affiliate Leadership Award. Karen is an Advisor to the Field's Institute/Palette Cybersecurity Advisory Board and offers mentorship and coaching to new and current cybersecurity practitioners.

MANSOUR KHAN

A high-profile and dedicated information security executive with a demonstrated record of success leading cross-functional, multi-cultural organizations within fast-paced, ever-changing environments. Mansour has a proven track record in information security, IT and risk management with diverse experience working in three different continents (North America, Europe, & Asia).

With over 25 years of experience, Mansour is an aggressive strategist and an implementer; he excels at supporting business execution strategies while successfully integrating information security and privacy strategies with business goals and objectives.

He has raised the Information Security posture of several organizations. In addition, he strongly believes that the success of any function lies with the existence of a strong team.

His ability to provide successful information security strategies come from years of knowledge and experience in Information Systems, Information Security, Risk Management, Corporate Security and Investigations, Privacy, Financial and Management Accounting, as well as Sales and overall Business Management. He has a strong understanding of Business, IT and Security/Risk management and has exceptional skills articulating the IT & Security risks to the business executives while translating the business needs and requirements to the technical team in order to deliver the desired business objectives.

INDEX

F

G

H

I

K

Q

CPSIA information can be obtained
at www.ICGtesting.com
Printed in the USA
BVHW042020261122
652819BV00001B/4